THE
TEX-MEX TABLE

60 KNOCKOUT RECIPES
FROM THE LONE STAR STATE

MANDI HICKMAN
Founder of Dash of Mandi

PAGE STREET
PUBLISHING CO.

PAGE STREET
PUBLISHING CO.

Copyright © 2021 Mandi Hickman

First published in 2021 by
Page Street Publishing Co.
27 Congress Street, Suite 105
Salem, MA 01970
www.pagestreetpublishing.com

Distributed by Macmillan, sales in Canada by The Canadian Manda Group.

25   24   23   22   21   1   2   3   4   5

ISBN-13: 978-1-64567-388-0
ISBN-10: 1-64567-388-X

Library of Congress Control Number: 2021931369

Cover and book design by Laura Benton for Page Street Publishing Co.
Photography by Mandi Hickman

Printed and bound in China

Dedication

To my mom and dad: Thank you for believing in me and always telling me I can do anything I set my mind to.

To my husband, Robbie: Thank you for being so supportive of my dreams every single day—and for being the taste tester for this cookbook.

CONTENTS

INTRODUCTION

Like most people, I've loved food my whole life. The cooking part came to me later, but I've always had an appetite for trying different things. I first learned how to cook when my husband, Robbie, and I moved to Houston, Texas, about six years ago. Something about moving far away from family, who all lived in New Jersey where I grew up, made me realize it was probably time I learned to cook for myself. The restaurants and food trucks in Houston were all so unique and they inspired me to get creative in the kitchen. I fell in love with creating my own recipes very quickly.

My husband and I only lived in Houston temporarily. A few years later, after moving around a bit, we ended up back in the Lone Star State, this time in Austin. I started to get serious about food blogging after that. It has been quite the journey. I can confidently say I'm almost always thinking about food and how I can create dishes with my own spin on them. The food scene here in Austin has always been my biggest inspiration. Everywhere you look, there is food! I spend a lot of time in the kitchen, but I always try to break it up with some dining out or takeout. Every time we try a delicious new dish from the Austin food scene, I tell my husband, "I need to try and re-create this at home." You'll find some of that inspiration in these recipes!

Because I'm from New Jersey, you're probably wondering . . . why a Tex-Mex–inspired cookbook? Well, I was very homesick my first few years in Texas. I missed my family and friends more than anything. When those waves of homesickness came crashing in, I found so much comfort in the food scene here. Fast forward a few years and now Texas truly feels like home to me—food and cooking were a big part of creating that feeling. When family comes into town, we take them all over the city to try our favorite taco spots, BBQ, southern comfort food or margaritas. It may not be the food I was surrounded with while I was growing up, but it has become my favorite by far. The people in Austin put a lot of passion into their food. They get up before the sun rises to smoke a brisket, they try to perfect their chili recipe for years and they sure know how to make a good taco.

Tex-Mex cuisine is vibrant, flavorful and fresh. It's comfort food that's made with love. It's simple but it makes people happy. You truly cannot be in a bad mood when you are presented with a margarita on the rocks, a taco platter and guacamole. It's impossible! Tex-Mex is good-mood food.

Enchiladas, nachos, queso, fajitas, margaritas and tacos of all sorts are just a handful of the dishes you will find in this cookbook. These recipes are the perfect blend of traditional and evolved. They're meant to bring people together. The best part is you can live anywhere and make and enjoy these Tex-Mex recipes. They're easy, attainable and, most importantly, delicious.

So, whether you say "y'all" or "yous guys," let's get cooking!

Mandy Hickman

TACOS & TORTILLA HANDHELDS

Here's an entire chapter dedicated to my favorite food of all time: TACOS (and of course all the other fun handheld options you can make with tortillas, like quesadillas, tostadas and taquitos). Most of us can agree that these dishes are full of flavor and just straight-up drool-worthy. But many of us also love them because of the various ways we can use them to make tortilla-based meals.

Tortillas should be a household staple because of their versatility. When it comes to tacos, the options are endless. You can do classic ground beef or succulent shrimp; blackened fish (page 13) or even simple grilled chicken (page 17). And don't even get me started with the toppings, which can sometimes be the best part! You can top these meals with so many different salsas, slaws or queso. Be sure to check out the tasty homemade topping recipes in The Best Salsas & Fixins chapter (page 101).

If you want to take a break from tacos and change it up, tostadas, quesadillas and taquitos are just as delicious and some of my favorite ways to use tortillas. It all depends on what you're craving. Tostadas are crunchy, quesadillas are warm and toasty and taquitos are crispy!

Tortilla-based dishes are everywhere you turn in Texas. In this chapter, I'm bringing all the flavors to you to make in your own kitchen. I hope you find a fun new recipe to add to your Taco (or Tortilla) Tuesday rotation.

EASY BREAKFAST TACOS

Breakfast tacos are a morning staple in Texas. I'd never had one until I moved to Texas, and now they're one of my favorite meals. Whenever I have my family or friends in town, we make sure to go out to get breakfast tacos at least once. The amazing thing is that they are so easy to make at home. They're the perfect breakfast for hosting, too! Bring a little bit of Texas to your morning routine with this line-up.

⧚ Yield: 8 tacos ⧚

1 lb (454 g) store-bought shredded hash browns

Oil of choice, for cooking the hash browns

4 slices of bacon

1 (4-oz [113-g]) can diced green chilis

8 eggs, whisked

½ cup (57 g) shredded pepper Jack cheese

8 flour tortillas, warmed

Pico de Gallo (page 109), for topping

In a large skillet over medium heat, cook the hash browns with a glug of oil until slightly browned, 5 to 8 minutes. Remove the hash browns from the pan and set aside.

In the same skillet, add the slices of bacon and cook over medium heat until crispy. This should only take a few minutes on each side. Remove the bacon and add it to a paper towel-lined plate.

Return the skillet to the heat, leaving the drippings or adding 1 tablespoon (15 ml) of the oil of your choice, and add the diced green chilis and sauté for about a minute.

Reduce the heat to medium-low and add the whisked eggs. When the eggs begin to set, add the shredded cheese. Stir the cheesy eggs around until they are cooked through and fluffy, 3 to 5 minutes.

Add a little bit of hash browns and eggs to each warmed tortilla. Break each piece of bacon in half, place one half of bacon in each taco and top with Pico de Gallo.

BLACKENED FISH TACOS

When I lived in New Jersey, my mom would always make blackened fish tacos with slaw for dinner. It was so simple and easy but we would always look forward to it! This recipe gives me coastal nostalgia for my home state, but with an added Texas flair thanks to the addition of my Chipotle Slaw (page 116). This recipe combines both of my homes in one comforting and delicious meal.

⋛ *Yield: 4–6 servings* ⋚

2 tsp (6 g) chili powder

2 tsp (4 g) ground cumin

1 tsp smoked paprika

1 tsp garlic powder

½ tsp onion powder

Pinch of cayenne, optional

1 tsp salt

½ tsp ground black pepper

1½ lb (680 g) mahi mahi fillets

2 tbsp (30 ml) olive oil

Juice of ½ lime

Chipotle Slaw (page 116)

8–10 flour tortillas, warmed

Pickled jalapeños, for topping

Chopped cilantro leaves, for topping

In a small mixing bowl, combine the chili powder, ground cumin, smoked paprika, garlic powder, onion powder, cayenne (if using), salt and pepper.

Pat the mahi mahi fillets dry and rub the seasoning on both sides of the fish.

Add the olive oil to a skillet over medium-high heat. When heated, add the fish and cook for 3 to 4 minutes per side, or until the fish is cooked through. The cook time will depend on how thick the fish fillets are.

Remove the fish from the skillet and break the fillets into smaller pieces for the tacos. Squeeze lime juice over the fish.

Assemble the tacos by adding a few spoonfuls (or more or less, depending on your preference) of the Chipotle Slaw to each warmed tortilla, followed by the mahi mahi. Top with the pickled jalapeños and chopped cilantro.

SLOW COOKER BARBACOA TACOS

Taco night is made easy with these barbacoa tacos. Throw everything in your slow cooker and let it do all the work for you. That's the beautiful thing about slow cooking. The meat turns out so juicy and packed with flavor. Add some shredded cabbage for a crunch, pickled red onion for a bite, some cheese and cilantro, and you have the perfect taco.

Yield: 6 servings

Barbacoa

3 lb (1.4 kg) beef brisket, trimmed and cut into 2- to 3-inch (5- to 8-cm) pieces

2 chipotle chilis in adobo sauce, chopped

1 tbsp (15 ml) adobo sauce

1 (4-oz [113-g]) can diced green chilis

½ cup (120 ml) beef broth

1 tbsp (15 ml) apple cider vinegar

3 cloves garlic, minced

2 tsp (2 g) dried oregano

1 tbsp (6 g) ground cumin

2 tsp (6 g) chili powder

2 bay leaves

Salt and pepper

Juice of ½ lime

Tacos

Warmed flour tortillas

Shredded cabbage, for topping

Crumbled cotija cheese or queso fresco, for topping

Quick Pickled Red Onions (page 110), for topping

Chopped cilantro, for topping

Add the brisket, chipotle chilis, adobo sauce, diced green chilis, beef broth, apple cider vinegar, garlic, dried oregano, ground cumin, chili powder, bay leaves and a generous sprinkle of salt and pepper to a slow cooker.

Cover and cook on high for 5 to 6 hours or low for 8 to 9 hours.

Using a slotted spoon, remove the bay leaves, then remove the brisket and shred the meat with two forks. After shredding, add the brisket back to the slow cooker.

Stir in the lime juice and give everything a good mix.

Serve the beef barbacoa on warmed tortillas with the shredded cabbage. Top with crumbled cotija or queso fresco, pickled red onions and chopped cilantro.

GRILLED CHICKEN STREET TACOS

These street tacos are so fun! I love serving them with mini corn tortillas. Street tacos are typically very simple and include a meat, onion, cilantro and lime. I put my own spin on them by chopping up my Quick Pickled Red Onions (page 110) for a topping. My Mango or Pineapple Salsa (page 102) is also a great addition that adds a perfect complement to the zesty marinade on the chicken, but feel free to leave it out if you want a simpler taco recipe.

Yield: 4–6 servings

4 oz (120 ml) pineapple juice

2 tbsp (30 ml) lime juice, from about 1 lime

2 tbsp (30 ml) apple cider vinegar

2 cloves garlic, minced

¼ cup (4 g) cilantro leaves, chopped

2 tsp (4 g) cumin

2 tsp (6 g) chipotle chili powder, or regular chili powder

½ tsp oregano

2 lb (907 g) chicken thighs, boneless and skinless

1 tsp salt

1 tsp pepper

Mini corn tortillas, or tortillas of choice

Quick Pickled Red Onions (page 110), chopped, for topping

Chopped cilantro, for topping

Crumbled cotija cheese, for topping

Mango or Pineapple Salsa (page 102), for topping

Hot sauce, for topping, optional

In a mixing bowl, combine the pineapple juice, lime juice, apple cider vinegar, garlic, cilantro, cumin, chipotle chili powder and oregano.

Season both sides of the chicken thighs with salt and pepper, then add them to a ziplock bag or air-tight container. Pour the marinade over the chicken and let it marinate in the refrigerator for 2 to 4 hours.

Preheat an outdoor grill to medium-high heat.

Grill the chicken for about 5 minutes per side or until the thighs are cooked through and the internal temperature hits 165°F (75°C). Remove the chicken from the grill and let it rest for 5 minutes, then cut the meat into small pieces.

Serve the chicken on tortillas with the pickled red onions, cilantro, cotija cheese and salsa. Drizzle with your favorite hot sauce, if desired.

CHOPPED BRISKET TACOS

This is by far my favorite way to use leftover smoked brisket from my Robbie's Smoked Brisket recipe (page 59). In Texas, a lot of people love adding a BBQ flair to their tacos. I've had quite a few chopped brisket tacos at various food trucks in Austin, and I've never had one that I didn't love. This recipe marries Texas and Mexican food so nicely to create the perfect Tex-Mex taco.

⋛ *Yield: 4 servings* ⋚

1 cup (240 ml) Easy Homemade BBQ Sauce (page 113)

½ tsp chipotle chili powder, optional

6–8 flour tortillas, warmed

3 cups (320 g) Robbie's Smoked Brisket (page 59), warmed and chopped into tiny pieces

Pickleback Slaw (page 119), for topping

To a small saucepan over medium-low heat, add the BBQ sauce. Stir in the chipotle chili powder, if desired. This will add some heat to your taco if you like a bit of spice. Let the mixture simmer for 5 to 7 minutes, stirring frequently.

Assemble your tacos by drizzling a little bit of BBQ sauce on the bottom of each tortilla. Top each tortilla with the chopped brisket and a healthy portion of the Pickleback Slaw.

PIMENTO CHEESE QUESADILLAS

Pimento cheese—one of the many things I never knew about until I moved to Texas. Now it's one of my favorite cheese dips. The classic southern pimento cheese dip is often served cold with crackers. However, everyone makes it differently. I love it as a hot dip (page 92) or in this case between a crispy tortilla for the perfect cheesy handheld meal.

Yield: 4 servings

1 cup (113 g) shredded sharp cheddar cheese

¼ cup (60 ml) mayonnaise

1 (4-oz [113-g]) can diced pimentos, drained

¼ tsp smoked paprika

¼ tsp ground mustard

Pinch of cayenne

Salt and pepper, to taste

4 (8-inch [20-cm]) flour tortillas

1 tbsp (15 ml) olive oil, divided

In a medium mixing bowl, combine the cheese, mayonnaise, pimentos, smoked paprika, ground mustard, cayenne, salt and pepper. Mix well.

Lay out the tortillas on a work surface and divide the cheese mixture evenly across half of each tortilla. Fold each tortilla in half, covering the cheese mixture.

Heat ½ tablespoon (8 ml) of the olive oil in a large skillet over medium heat. Add two of the folded tortillas to the skillet.

Cook the quesadillas for 2 to 3 minutes per side or until the tortillas are browned and crispy on each side. Set aside the cooked quesadillas and repeat with the other two tortillas.

Slice each quesadilla in half and enjoy!

PULLED PORK QUESADILLAS

Making pulled pork (page 60) often leaves you with some leftovers. I love using the leftovers for nachos, tacos and, of course, this Texas-inspired quesadilla. It's simple, easy and absolutely delicious. The succulent barbecue pulled pork, spicy pickled jalapeños and melty Monterey Jack all come together perfectly in a toasty quesadilla. This quesadilla is the perfect example of how combining quintessential Texas BBQ with staples of Mexican cuisine can give you such a delicious recipe.

Yield: 4 servings

1 cup (225 g) Pellet Grill Pulled Pork (page 60)

¼ cup (60 ml) Easy Homemade BBQ Sauce (page 113)

4 (8-inch [20-cm]) flour tortillas

½ cup (57 g) shredded Monterey Jack cheese

Pickled jalapeños, to taste

1 tbsp (15 ml) olive oil, divided

In a medium mixing bowl, combine the pulled pork and barbecue sauce. Mix well.

Lay out the tortillas on a work surface and divide the cheese evenly across half of each tortilla. Add ¼ cup (56 g) of barbecue pulled pork on top of the cheese. Top each portion with your desired amount of pickled jalapeños and fold the tortillas over.

Heat ½ tablespoon (8 ml) of olive oil in a large skillet over medium heat. Add two of the folded tortillas to the skillet. Cook the quesadillas for 2 to 3 minutes per side, or until the tortillas are browned and crispy on each side.

Set aside the cooked quesadillas and repeat with the other two tortillas.

Slice each quesadilla in half and enjoy!

LOADED BREAKFAST BURRITOS

A breakfast burrito is one of the most filling and satisfying breakfast foods out there.
Pro tip: Prep a bunch of these ahead of time and store them in the refrigerator or freezer
(see Note). Then all you have to do is heat them up in the oven and you have a quick,
easy and delicious breakfast in no time. You'll love adding some spicy
Tex-Mex flair to your mornings!

Yield: 2 burritos

1 tbsp (15 ml) butter or olive oil

5 eggs, whisked

Salt and pepper

1 cup (113 g) shredded Monterey Jack cheese

2 burrito-sized flour tortillas

1 cup (230 g) refried beans, heated

1 avocado, sliced (see Note)

⅓ cup (80 ml) Pico de Gallo (page 109)

Hot sauce, for topping

In a large skillet over medium heat, add the butter or oil and heat for 30 seconds. When heated, pour the eggs into the skillet and season with a pinch of salt and pepper.

When the eggs begin to set, add the shredded cheese. Stir the mixture around until the eggs are cooked through and fluffy, 3 to 5 minutes.

Remove the cheesy eggs from the heat and set them aside.

Heat the tortillas in the same skillet for about 1 minute per side. You can also heat them up in the microwave if you prefer.

Assemble the burritos by dividing the refried beans, cheesy scrambled eggs, avocado and Pico de Gallo among the two tortillas. Place everything in the center of the tortilla with plenty of room above and below for folding.

Fold the left and right sides of the tortilla over the filling. Then carefully fold the bottom of the tortilla up and over the filling. Tuck the sides and filling as you roll upward so that it's a nice, neat burrito. Repeat with the other burrito.

Wrap each burrito with foil and slice it in half. Serve with hot sauce drizzled on top.

You can store these burritos in the refrigerator for 2 days or the freezer for 2 months. To reheat frozen burritos, bake them at 425°F (220°C) for 15 to 20 minutes, flipping halfway through the baking time.

NOTE: If you plan to freeze these burritos, leave out the avocado.

ANGRY TUNA MELT TOSTADAS

This is not a traditional tuna melt, nor a traditional tostada. But, when the two come together you get the easiest weeknight dinner ever. These spicy and crispy tuna melts are one of my favorite meals to make when I don't want to spend a whole lot of time cooking or doing dishes. I love marrying the Americanized tuna melt with some Mexican spices and flair.

⋛ *Yield: 3 servings* ⋚

3 flour tortillas

2 (5-oz [142-g]) cans tuna, drained

¼ cup (60 ml) mayonnaise

1 tbsp (15 ml) hot sauce (I like Frank's RedHot)

1 tsp smoked paprika

Pinch of garlic powder

Pinch of cayenne

Salt and pepper, to taste

¼ cup (70 g) pickled jalapeños, roughly chopped

¼ cup (28 g) shredded pepper Jack cheese

Chopped cilantro, for garnish, optional

Preheat the oven to 400°F (200°C).

Spray both sides of the tortillas with nonstick cooking spray, then place them in a single layer on a baking sheet and bake for 5 minutes.

Meanwhile, in a small mixing bowl, combine the tuna, mayonnaise, hot sauce, smoked paprika, garlic powder, cayenne, salt, pepper and pickled jalapeños.

Remove the tortillas from the oven and top each one with one-third of the tuna mixture. Sprinkle the cheese over the tuna mixture. Bake the tostadas again for 6 to 7 minutes, or until the cheese has melted and is beginning to crisp up.

Top with chopped cilantro, if desired, and slice each tostada into four slices.

SHRIMP CEVICHE TOSTADAS

Shrimp ceviche is a refreshing cold dip that's usually served with chips. The first time I tried it was in Galveston, so now when I eat it, it reminds me of coastal Texas. I loved it so much that I wanted to make it into a full meal using crispy homemade tostadas. This vibrant meal is so light and fresh yet satisfying. The layer of smashed avocado between the tostada and the ceviche really brings it all together so nicely.

Yield: 4–6 servings

1 lb (454 g) shrimp, peeled, deveined, tails removed

½ cup (120 ml) lime juice, from about 6 limes

2 tbsp (30 ml) lemon juice

1 tbsp (15 ml) olive oil

Salt, to taste

½ cup (58 g) red onion, diced

1 jalapeño, seeds removed for mild spice, finely diced

1 Roma tomato, diced

¼ cup (4 g) cilantro, chopped

½ cup (68 g) sweet corn kernels, fresh or frozen and thawed

8 tsp (40 ml) frying oil, divided

8 corn tortillas

2 large ripe avocados

Pepper, to taste

Bring a large pot of water to a boil. Prepare a large bowl filled with ice water.

Add the shrimp to the boiling water and cook for 1 to 2 minutes, or until the shrimp are cooked through and turn a light pink color. Remove the shrimp from the pot and add them to the ice bath so they don't continue to cook.

After a minute or two, remove the shrimp from the ice bath and cut them into bite-sized pieces.

In a large mixing bowl, combine the chopped shrimp with the lime juice, lemon juice, olive oil and salt. Let the mixture marinate in the refrigerator for 30 minutes.

After 30 minutes, add the red onion, jalapeño, tomato, cilantro and corn to the bowl. Marinate in the refrigerator for another 20 minutes.

Meanwhile, make the tostadas. Heat a skillet over medium heat, add 1 teaspoon of oil and add one tortilla to the pan. Cook the tortillas, one at a time, on both sides until they are crispy. Repeat the process, adding a teaspoon of oil for each tortilla.

In a small mixing bowl, smash the avocados and season with a pinch of salt and pepper.

Spread a small layer of avocado on each tortilla and top with the shrimp ceviche.

TEX-MEX MEATS
& MAINS

The main course. Everything in this chapter is heavily inspired by the Tex-Mex flavors I've come across living in Texas. Some may be more traditional, while others have my own creative spin on them.

Barbacoa Burrito Bowls (page 39) and Easy Posole Verde (page 43) are classics. However, my Tex-Mex Meatballs & Rice (page 32) and Turkey Taco Skillet (page 35) might be something new you'll want to add to the dinner menu!

This chapter includes a variety of cooking methods, from one-pan meals and hearty soups to grilled meats packed with flavor, and the recipes highlight an array of proteins like beef, chicken and turkey. There is sure to be something in here for any occasion or craving!

TEX-MEX MEATBALLS & RICE

This one-pan meal is perfect for your weeknight dinner line-up. Chicken meatballs and fluffy rice are smothered in enchilada sauce and cheese. Meatballs are such a versatile meal. You can really make them to fit any cuisine. This Tex-Mex–inspired version is vibrant, drool-worthy and only uses one skillet.

Yield: 4 servings

1 lb (454 g) ground chicken

1 egg, whisked

½ cup (54 g) breadcrumbs

⅓ cup (53 g) finely chopped yellow onion

2 cloves garlic, minced

½ tsp salt

Pinch of ground black pepper

½ tsp ground cumin

½ tsp chili powder

¼ tsp dried oregano

1 tbsp (15 ml) olive oil

15 oz (445 ml) red enchilada sauce

1 cup (200 g) uncooked white rice

1 cup (113 g) shredded Mexican cheese

1 tbsp (1 g) chopped cilantro

In a medium-sized mixing bowl, combine the ground chicken, egg, bread-crumbs, onion, garlic, salt, pepper, cumin, chili powder and oregano. Mix to combine.

Using a cookie scoop or clean hands, form the mixture into round balls using about 1½ tablespoons (23 g) of the chicken mixture per meatball.

Heat the oil in a large skillet over medium heat, then add the meatballs in a single layer. Let them cook for about 3 minutes per side, for 6 minutes total.

Add the enchilada sauce and rice to the pan with the meatballs.

Reduce the heat to medium-low and cover the skillet with a lid. Let the meatballs and rice simmer for 18 to 20 minutes.

Remove the lid, sprinkle the shredded cheese on top then cover the pan with the lid again and let everything cook for an additional 2 to 3 minutes, or until the cheese is melted.

Top the meatballs and rice with the chopped cilantro and serve.

TURKEY TACO SKILLET

Easy, delicious, healthy and all made in one pan. This meal really checks all the boxes.
It's basically a deconstructed taco. I love making this dish and serving it with a bunch of
fun toppings. My husband loves it with sour cream and I love it with avocado and Quick
Pickled Red Onions (page 110). Just like tacos, you can top it however you please!

Yield: 4 servings

1 tbsp (15 ml) olive oil

1 yellow onion, finely chopped

1 jalapeño, seeds removed
and diced

1 lb (454 g) ground turkey

Salt and pepper

1 tbsp (8 g) chili powder

1 tsp smoked paprika

1 tsp ground cumin

¼ tsp cayenne

1 (15-oz [425-g]) can pinto beans,
drained and rinsed

1 cup (136 g) corn kernels, fresh or
frozen and thawed

12 oz (340 g) salsa, about 1 jar

4 oz (113 g) tortilla chips, about half
a large bag

1 cup (113 g) shredded Mexican
cheese blend

Chopped cilantro, for topping

Quick Pickled Red Onions
(page 110), for topping

Chopped tomatoes, for topping

Sliced avocado or Smashed
Guacamole (page 105), for topping

Sour cream, for topping

Lime wedges, for topping

In a large skillet over medium heat, warm the olive oil. When heated, add the
onion and jalapeño and sauté for 2 to 3 minutes.

Add the ground turkey and season with a generous sprinkle of salt and
pepper. Cook the turkey until it is browned, crumbling the meat into small
pieces as it cooks.

Add the chili powder, smoked paprika, cumin, cayenne, pinto beans, corn
and salsa. Mix well. Let the mixture cook for 3 minutes.

Lightly crumble the chips over the top of the turkey, then sprinkle the cheese
over the top of the chips. Cover the turkey skillet with a lid and let it cook for
1 to 2 minutes, or until the cheese melts.

Remove the pan from the heat and top the turkey skillet with chopped
cilantro, pickled red onions, chopped tomatoes, avocado or guacamole,
sour cream and lime wedges.

CHIPOTLE-AGAVE CHICKEN

These chicken thighs marinated in a sweet, smoky and tangy chipotle-agave barbecue sauce are perfect for throwing on the grill. Serve them with a side of grilled veggies or slice them up and eat them in tacos. My fresh Mango or Pineapple Salsa (page 102) would also go great with this chicken. It's the ideal meal for a hot summer day in Texas, or just about anywhere.

⋝ *Yield: 4 servings* ⋜

2 chipotles in adobo sauce

1 tbsp (15 ml) adobo sauce

¼ cup (60 ml) agave

¾ cup (180 ml) Easy Homemade BBQ Sauce (page 113)

1 clove garlic, minced

½ tsp ground cumin

Salt and pepper, to taste

2 lb (907 g) chicken thighs, boneless and skinless

In a blender or food processor, combine the chipotles, adobo sauce, agave, barbecue sauce, garlic, cumin, salt and pepper. Blend until smooth.

Add the chicken thighs to an airtight container with a lid or a resealable bag. Add the chipotle barbecue sauce and make sure the chicken is fully coated in the sauce.

Marinate the chicken in the refrigerator for 2 to 6 hours.

Heat an outdoor grill to medium-high heat. Grill the chicken for 5 minutes on each side or until the internal temperature reaches 165°F (75°C).

Remove the chicken from the grill and let it rest for 5 to 7 minutes before slicing.

BARBACOA BURRITO BOWLS

My Slow Cooker Barbacoa Tacos recipe (page 14) can make more than just tacos! These burrito bowls are another great option. They're incredibly satisfying and customizable. If you're hosting a gathering, this would be a great dish to serve. Spread out all the toppings and let everyone build their own bowl. Pair them with Mexican Martinis (page 139) and you have yourself the perfect meal.

⋛ Yield: 4 servings ⋜

2 cups (400 g) Tex-Mex Fried Rice (page 124)

2 cups (242 g) barbacoa (page 14)

1 cup (240 g) Pico de Gallo (page 109)

1 (16-oz [454-g]) can pinto beans, drained, rinsed and heated

1 avocado, thinly sliced

½ cup (120 ml) sour cream, or to taste

¼ cup (70 g) Quick Pickled Red Onions (page 110)

Pickled jalapeños, to taste, optional

¼ cup (4 g) chopped cilantro

1 lime, cut into wedges

Reheat the Tex-Mex Fried Rice and barbacoa. You can do this by microwaving in 30-second intervals until heated through, or you can add them to a skillet over medium heat and cook until warmed, 5 to 7 minutes.

Assemble your bowls by adding ½ cup (100 g) of rice to each bowl. Top with ½ cup (60 g) of barbacoa and ¼ cup (60 g) of Pico de Gallo.

Add your desired amount of beans, avocado and sour cream to each bowl. Top with the pickled red onions, pickled jalapeños, if desired, and chopped cilantro.

Serve with some lime wedges on the side.

FLANK STEAK WITH JALAPEÑO PESTO

I love making this dish with my husband. I marinate the steak and make the jalapeño pesto, then he takes care of the grilling. Cut the recipe in half and it makes for the perfect date-night-at-home dinner. Or impress your guests by whipping it up for them. It's elevated but also so easy. You'll love the marinated steak paired with my spicy take on pesto!

Yield: 4 servings

Flank Steak

½ cup (120 ml) olive oil

2 tbsp (30 ml) lime juice

2 tbsp (30 ml) Worcestershire sauce

2 tbsp (28 g) brown sugar

2 tbsp (30 ml) red wine vinegar

1 tsp garlic powder

3 tsp (9 g) chili powder

1 tsp onion powder

1 tsp cumin

½ tsp paprika

½ tsp dried oregano

2 lb (907 g) flank steak

Salt and pepper

Jalapeño Pesto

⅓ cup (45 g) pine nuts

1 bunch cilantro, stems removed

1 jalapeño, seeds removed for less heat

1 clove garlic

1 tbsp (15 ml) lime juice

⅓ cup (80 ml) olive oil

¼ cup (30 g) crumbled cotija cheese

Salt and pepper, to taste

In a mixing bowl, combine the olive oil, lime juice, Worcestershire sauce, brown sugar, red wine vinegar, garlic powder, chili powder, onion powder, cumin, paprika and oregano.

Season both sides of the flank steak with a sprinkle of salt and pepper.

Add the steaks to a large ziplock bag and pour in the marinade. Let the steaks marinate in the refrigerator for at least 2 hours.

To make the jalapeño pesto, combine the pine nuts, cilantro, jalapeño, garlic, lime juice, olive oil, cotija, salt and pepper in a food processor or blender and blend until smooth. Cover and refrigerate until ready to use.

Preheat an outdoor grill to medium-high.

Grill the steaks for 5 to 6 minutes per side, or until a meat thermometer reads 130 to 135°F (54 to 57°C) for medium-rare.

Remove the steaks from the grill and let them rest for 10 minutes before slicing. Serve with the jalapeño pesto.

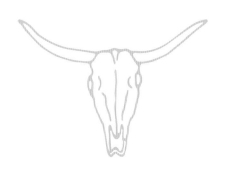

EASY POSOLE VERDE

Posole is a traditional Mexican soup that I discovered while living in Texas. If I see it on a menu at a restaurant in Austin, I get it every time. Made with hominy and meat, it's so comforting and flavorful. I garnish this soup with all the classics: shredded cabbage, sliced radishes, jalapeño slices, cilantro and lime. My version is super simple and comes together in no time! It's the perfect cozy meal.

Yield: 4–6 servings

1 tbsp (15 ml) olive oil

2 cloves garlic, minced

1 (25-oz [708-g]) can hominy, drained and rinsed

2 (4-oz [113-g]) cans diced green chilis

6 cups (1.4 L) chicken stock

1 cup (136 g) corn kernels, fresh or frozen and thawed

⅔ cup (160 g) Tomatillo Salsa Verde (page 106), or store bought

2 tsp (4 g) ground cumin

1 tsp dried oregano

Salt and pepper, to taste

1 lb (454 g) chicken breast

Juice of ½ lime

Lime wedges, for topping

Sliced radish, for topping

Shredded cabbage, for topping, optional

Chopped cilantro, for topping

Sliced jalapeño, for topping

Heat the olive oil in a large soup pot over medium heat. Add the garlic and cook for 1 minute, stirring frequently.

Add the hominy, green chilis, chicken stock, corn, salsa verde, cumin, oregano, salt and pepper. Add the chicken breasts and push them down into the soup, making sure they are completely covered by the rest of the ingredients.

Bring the soup to a boil then reduce the heat to medium-low and let it simmer uncovered for 20 to 25 minutes.

Remove the chicken from the soup and shred it with two forks. Add the shredded chicken back to the pot and stir in the lime juice.

Ladle the posole verde into soup bowls and add your desired toppings—I recommend using all of them!

CREAMY CHICKEN ENCHILADA SOUP

This dish has all the delicious flavors of chicken enchiladas in one cozy soup. I'm a huge fan of making a big pot of soup in the winter. It's easy and it makes for great leftovers! This one is bursting with fun and unique Tex-Mex components. I always top mine with shredded cheese and tortilla strips. It's the ultimate comfort food!

⋛ Yield: 5–6 servings ⋚

1 tbsp (15 ml) olive oil

1 yellow onion, finely chopped

3 cloves garlic, minced

1 lb (454 g) chicken breast, boneless and skinless

1 cup (136 g) corn kernels, fresh or frozen and thawed

1 (4-oz [113-g]) can diced green chilis

1 (15-oz [425-g]) can black beans, drained and rinsed

1 (19-oz [562-ml]) can red enchilada sauce

4 cups (960 ml) chicken stock

2 tsp (4 g) ground cumin

¼ tsp dried oregano

¼ tsp cayenne

1 tsp salt

½ tsp ground black pepper

½ cup (120 ml) sour cream

Juice of 1 lime

Tortilla strips, for topping

Chopped cilantro or sliced green onion, for topping

Shredded Mexican cheese, for topping

Sliced jalapeño, for topping, optional

In a large pot over medium heat, warm the olive oil. Add the onion and sauté for 5 minutes, stirring occasionally. Add the garlic and cook for 1 minute, stirring frequently.

Add the chicken, corn, diced green chilis, black beans, enchilada sauce, chicken stock, cumin, oregano, cayenne, salt and pepper to the pot.

Bring the soup to a boil then reduce the heat to medium-low and let simmer uncovered for 20 to 25 minutes, or until the chicken is cooked through and no pink remains.

Remove the chicken from the pot and shred it with two forks. Add the shredded chicken back to the pot and stir in the sour cream and lime juice. Let the soup simmer for an additional 5 minutes to let the flavors meld.

Ladle the soup into bowls and top each serving with tortilla strips, chopped cilantro or sliced green onion, shredded cheese and sliced jalapeño, if desired.

BBQ & OTHER LONE STAR CLASSICS

This chapter is heavier on the Texas side of things. These BBQ-inspired recipes can be smoked on your grill or smothered in BBQ sauce like Robbie's Smoked Brisket (page 59) or can be made into Texas Chili (page 52), ribs (page 56) or pulled pork (page 60). These recipes are hearty, filling and packed with flavor—just like most of the food you find here in Texas!

Some recipes in this chapter are a little more time-consuming than others, but all of them are easy enough! They were all created with love and meant to bring a little taste of Texas to you wherever you may be.

We can't all be ultimate pit masters like Aaron Franklin (owner of Franklin Barbecue here in Austin), but that doesn't mean we can't make delicious BBQ meat-inspired recipes in our own home. Or in some cases, our own backyard.

BAKED BOURBON BARBECUE WINGS

This is my fool-proof oven-baked chicken wing recipe. The key to getting them super crispy is placing them on a wire rack with some space in between the wings. Combine your favorite bourbon and my Easy Homemade BBQ Sauce (page 113) for a flavor-packed, Texas-inspired sauce.

Yield: 3–4 servings

2 lb (907 g) split chicken wings

1 tbsp (15 ml) olive oil

1 tsp salt

½ tsp ground black pepper

1 tbsp (14 g) brown sugar

¾ cup (180 ml) Easy Homemade BBQ Sauce (page 113)

¼ cup (60 ml) good-quality bourbon

Preheat the oven to 400°F (200°C). Line a large baking sheet with foil, then top with a wire cooling rack.

Pat the chicken wings dry, then add them to a large mixing bowl and toss with the olive oil, salt, pepper and brown sugar.

Place the chicken wings on the wire rack and leave some space in between each wing. This helps them get crispy!

Transfer the chicken wings to the oven and bake for 35 to 40 minutes, flipping them with tongs halfway through. They should be nice and crispy by the end.

While the wings bake, in a large mixing bowl, combine the barbecue sauce and bourbon. Mix well.

Remove the wings from the oven and place the wings in the mixing bowl with the barbecue sauce and bourbon combo. Set the baking sheet aside. Toss the wings in the sauce to fully coat.

Transfer the coated wings back to the wire rack–lined baking sheet and bake for 5 more minutes.

Serve immediately and enjoy!

SMOKED PEACH BARBECUE WINGS

This peach barbecue sauce is incredibly easy and is perfect on some crispy smoked chicken wings. If you don't own a pellet grill, feel free to follow the baked chicken wing method for my Baked Bourbon Barbecue Wings on page 48. They will still be delicious! Texas has great peaches and great barbecue sauce. So, why not combine the two and smother it on some smoked chicken wings?

Yield: 3–4 servings

2 lb (907 g) split chicken wings

2 tbsp (30 ml) olive oil

2 tsp (12 g) salt

1 tsp ground black pepper

¾ cup (180 ml) Easy Homemade BBQ Sauce (page 113)

½ cup (160 g) peach preserves

Preheat a pellet grill to 350°F (175°C).

Pat the chicken wings dry and add them to a large mixing bowl with the olive oil, salt and pepper. Mix well.

Place the chicken wings on the grill and close the lid. Let the wings cook for 40 minutes or until they are crispy, turning them once about halfway through the cooking time.

While the wings are cooking, combine the barbecue sauce and peach preserves in a large mixing bowl. Make sure the bowl is large enough to fit the chicken wings, too!

Remove the chicken wings from the grill and toss them with the barbecue sauce and peach preserves. Place the coated chicken wings back on the grill and let cook for an additional 2 to 3 minutes per side. This will lock in all those sweet flavors.

Remove the wings from the grill and serve.

TEXAS CHILI

Chili is the first thing I crave when the temperature starts to drop. I've learned that beans are sometimes (usually) frowned upon in Texas chili recipes. I've talked to a few native Texans about this. I've been told that chili is a big part of cook-offs and competitions and the beans are considered "fillers." They want to focus on the flavor of the meat and seasonings. However, a lot of Texans also told me they still add beans to their homemade chili. So, I'll leave it up to you—hence the optional beans in the ingredients list.

⸎ Yield: 4–5 servings ⸎

3–4 lb (1.4–1.8 kg) boneless chuck roast, excess fat removed, cut into 1-inch (2.5-cm) pieces

Salt and pepper

4 tbsp (60 ml) olive oil, divided

1 poblano pepper, seeds removed and chopped

1 jalapeño, seeds removed and finely chopped

1 yellow onion, chopped

1 tbsp (14 g) brown sugar

2 tbsp (16 g) chili powder, or more to taste

2 tbsp (12 g) ground cumin

2 tsp (6 g) smoked paprika

1 tsp dried oregano

4 cloves garlic, minced

2 tbsp (32 g) tomato paste

4 cups (960 ml) beef broth

1 tbsp (15 ml) Worcestershire sauce

1 (15-oz [425-g]) can pinto beans, drained and rinsed, optional

2 bay leaves

Shredded cheddar cheese, for topping

Sliced green onions, for topping

Sour cream, for topping, optional

Liberally season the chuck roast pieces with salt and pepper.

Heat 2 tablespoons (30 ml) of the olive oil in a large pot over medium-high heat. Add the meat in batches and cook until browned. Remove the meat when browned and set aside.

Add the remaining 2 tablespoons (30 ml) of the olive oil to the pot with the poblano pepper, jalapeño and onion. Let the veggies cook for about 6 minutes, stirring occasionally.

Add the brown sugar, chili powder, cumin, smoked paprika, oregano, salt and pepper to taste and garlic to the cooked peppers and onion. Let the mixture cook for 1 minute, stirring frequently.

Add the meat back to the pot along with the tomato paste, beef broth, Worcestershire sauce, beans (if using) and bay leaves. Bring everything to a boil then reduce the heat to medium-low and let it simmer for 2 to 2½ hours, stirring occasionally.

Taste and adjust the seasonings if necessary. Remove the bay leaves.

Ladle the chili into bowls and add your shredded cheddar, sliced green onion and sour cream, if desired.

FRITO PIE

Frito pie is a popular Texas snack served from a truck at football games, rodeos or festivals. It's simply a bag of Fritos® topped with chili and whatever other tasty toppings they have to offer. I love making it at home with a big batch of chili, shredded cheddar cheese, sour cream and sliced green onion. Any corn chip will do, not just Fritos!

Yield: 6 servings

1 batch of Texas Chili (page 52)

6 cups (225 g) Fritos original corn chips, or corn chip of choice

2 cups (226 g) shredded sharp cheddar cheese

¼ cup (12 g) sliced green onions

Sour cream, for topping

Sliced jalapeños, for topping, optional

Chopped tomatoes, for topping, optional

To a large soup pot over medium heat, add the chili. Let it simmer until heated through, stirring occasionally, 10 to 15 minutes.

Assemble the Frito pie in bowls by adding a layer of Fritos followed by a hearty portion of chili. You can also cut open a bag of Fritos at the top and add the chili on top. This is how they do it in the food trucks!

Sprinkle the Frito pie with cheddar cheese and sliced green onions. Top with sour cream, sliced jalapeños and chopped tomatoes, if desired.

BAKED STRAWBERRY BARBECUE RIBS

Everyone loves smoked ribs in Texas. However, I know not everyone has access to a smoker. The cool thing is that you can still make killer ribs in the oven! This method is foolproof. It's easy and the ribs come out fall-off-the-bone tender every time. The strawberry barbecue sauce is the perfect sweet and tangy combination. My husband devours these ribs every time I make them!

Yield: 4–5 servings

2½ lb (1.1 kg) baby back ribs

2 tbsp (30 ml) apple cider vinegar

2 tbsp (27 g) brown sugar

1 tbsp (7 g) smoked paprika

2 tsp (10 g) garlic powder

2 tsp (12 g) salt

1 tsp ground black pepper

1 cup (240 ml) Easy Homemade BBQ Sauce (page 113)

⅓ cup (95 g) strawberry preserves

Preheat the oven to 300°F (150°C) and line a large baking sheet with foil.

Place the ribs on a cutting board and remove the silver membrane by carefully using a butter knife and getting it under the membrane.

Place the ribs on the prepared baking sheet and brush both sides with the apple cider vinegar. Let the ribs sit for 20 minutes.

In a small mixing bowl, combine the brown sugar, smoked paprika, garlic powder, salt and pepper. Rub the seasoning mixture on both sides of the ribs to coat.

Wrap the ribs in foil and bake for 2 to 2½ hours, or until they become fork tender. Uncover the ribs for the last 20 minutes of cook time.

In a small mixing bowl, combine the barbecue sauce with the strawberry preserves. Remove the ribs from the oven and brush the strawberry barbecue sauce on both sides of the ribs. They should be fully coated.

Bake the coated ribs for 15 to 20 more minutes, then turn your broiler to high, and broil them for 1 to 2 minutes.

Cut, serve and enjoy!

ROBBIE'S SMOKED BRISKET

Smoked brisket is a big deal in Texas, and it's no wonder why. This tender, succulent Texas staple is full of comforting and delicious flavors. My husband recently got a pellet grill and his new hobby is smoking brisket, pork, wings and whatever else he can. He makes this brisket recipe for us quite a bit. It's an all-day thing, so you have to be prepared! However, the result is always worth the time. Slice the brisket and serve it with your favorite barbecue sauce or, my personal favorite, in my Chopped Brisket Tacos (page 18).

⊰ *Yield: 8 servings* ⊱

9–10 lb (4.1–4.5 kg) beef brisket, trimmed

¼ cup (28 g) coarse black pepper

¼ cup (80 g) Morton's salt

2 tbsp (28 g) brown sugar

1 tbsp (5 g) cayenne

1 tbsp (8 g) garlic powder

3–4 tbsp (45–60 ml) yellow mustard

Apple cider vinegar, as needed

Remove the brisket from the refrigerator 1 hour before you want to put it on the grill.

In a small mixing bowl or seasoning container, combine the pepper, salt, brown sugar, cayenne and garlic powder.

Slather the entire brisket with the yellow mustard then add the rub to all sides.

Preheat a pellet grill to 275°F (135°C).

Put the brisket on the top rack of your pellet grill (fat side up) and a tin tray full of water on the bottom rack. Prep a spray bottle with one part apple cider vinegar and one part water.

Let the brisket cook for 3 hours uninterrupted. Open the pellet grill and check the brisket. If it looks dry, spray it with the apple cider vinegar mix.

Check on the brisket every 30 to 45 minutes after the first 3 hours, spraying the brisket whenever it looks dry and topping off the water tray if it gets low.

When the internal temperature of the brisket reaches 190°F (88°C), remove it from the grill. Spray the brisket with the apple cider vinegar mixture, wrap it in foil and place it back on the grill until the internal temperature reaches 205°F (96°C).

Remove the brisket from the heat and let it rest for 1 to 2 hours before slicing.

PELLET GRILL PULLED PORK

This is another one of my husband's recipes. This pulled pork is so versatile! Add it to a sandwich or taco with barbecue sauce, or simply serve it up with some slaw and you've got a great meal. You can even add it to some nachos for the ultimate Tex-Mex experience! But, my personal favorite is using it to make my Pulled Pork Quesadillas on page 22.

⋛ *Yield: 8–10 servings* ⋚

1 tbsp (18 g) Morton's salt

1 tbsp (6 g) coarse black pepper

1 tsp garlic powder

1 tsp paprika

1 tsp onion powder

4 lb (1.8 kg) pork butt

2 tbsp (30 ml) yellow mustard

Apple cider vinegar, as needed

Preheat a pellet grill to 225°F (107°C).

In a small mixing bowl or seasoning container, mix the salt, pepper, garlic powder, paprika and onion powder.

Slather the pork butt with the yellow mustard on all sides then coat it evenly with the dry rub.

Wrap the pork butt in tin foil and place it on the top rack of the pellet grill. Add a tin tray of water to the bottom rack. Insert a temperature probe in the meat. Prep a spray bottle with one part apple cider vinegar and one part water.

Let the pork cook for 2 hours uninterrupted. Open your grill, unwrap the pork butt and quickly spray the meat with the apple cider vinegar mixture. Then rewrap the meat in the tin foil.

Then, let the pork cook until it reaches an internal temperature of 200°F (93°C), which should take about 6 hours. Quickly unwrap the meat, spray with the apple cider vinegar mixture and rewrap every hour.

Remove the pork from the grill and let it rest for 2 hours in the tin foil.

Remove the pork from the tin foil, shred the meat with two forks or your hands and serve.

OVEN MEALS WITH
TEX-MEX FLAIR

Oven meals are my jam: casseroles, sheet-pan meals, enchiladas. These recipes require little prep and little cleanup but give you amazing food to put on the table.

This chapter is for busy people who want to make a homemade dinner but don't have hours upon hours to spend in the kitchen. The best part is we don't have to sacrifice flavor here. That's the beauty of Tex-Mex. It can be effortless but it will still be packed with great taste and spice.

Some of my favorites from this chapter are the Sheet-Pan Chicken Fajitas with Jalapeño Sauce (page 69) and Fiesta Casserole (page 77). They're both incredibly easy but also satisfying, filling and delicious.

CHICKEN, SPINACH & ARTICHOKE ENCHILADAS

Enchiladas are a classic Tex-Mex dish. You can make them a number of ways . . . red, green, beef, chicken, seafood. However, I love this combination of shredded chicken (use rotisserie chicken to make life easier), spinach and artichokes to give a unique taste inspired by the classic American dip so many of us love!

⋛ Yield: 4 servings ⋜

1 tbsp (15 ml) olive oil

1 yellow onion, chopped

3 cups (85 g) baby spinach

1 (14-oz [397-g]) can artichoke hearts, drained very well and chopped

1 (4-oz [113-g]) can diced green chilis

2 cups (280 g) shredded cooked chicken

2 tsp (6 g) chili powder

1 tsp ground cumin

½ tsp smoked paprika

1 tsp garlic powder

Salt and pepper, to taste

¼ cup (60 ml) sour cream, plus more for topping, optional

8 flour tortillas

1 cup (240 ml) green enchilada sauce (Tomatillo Salsa Verde [page 106] will also work)

1 cup (113 g) shredded pepper Jack cheese

Chopped cilantro, for topping

Pickled jalapeños, for topping

Lime wedges, for topping

Preheat the oven to 400°F (200°C) and spray a 9 x 13-inch (23 x 33-cm) baking dish with nonstick cooking spray.

In a skillet over medium heat, warm the olive oil. When the oil is heated, add the onion and sauté for 4 minutes. Then add the spinach, artichokes and green chilis. Cook until the spinach is wilted, stirring periodically.

Add the cooked veggies to a large mixing bowl. Mix in the shredded chicken, chili powder, cumin, smoked paprika, garlic powder, salt, pepper and sour cream.

Assemble the enchiladas by adding a little bit of the chicken mixture in a tortilla, rolling it up tightly and placing the enchilada in the baking dish folded side down. Repeat with all of the tortillas. If there's leftover filling, add it to the baking dish.

Spray the top of the enchiladas with nonstick cooking spray and bake for 5 minutes.

Remove the enchiladas from the oven and pour the green enchilada sauce on top to coat, then sprinkle on the shredded cheese. Bake for 15 to 18 minutes.

Let the enchiladas cool for 10 minutes before serving. Trust me on this!

Serve with cilantro, pickled jalapeños, lime wedges and sour cream, if desired.

POBLANO & CORN ENCHILADAS

These vegetarian enchiladas are loaded with poblano pepper, onion, chilis, corn and beans. My husband hardly ever craves a meatless meal but he raves about these! The homemade enchilada sauce definitely adds a little something. However, I'm all about convenience and I know there are some good store-bought enchilada sauces out there. So, feel free to skip the homemade sauce step if you're looking for an even easier meal.

Yield: 4 servings

Enchilada Sauce

2 tbsp (30 ml) olive oil

2 tbsp (16 g) all-purpose flour

2 tbsp (16 g) chili powder

1 tsp ground cumin

1 tsp garlic powder

½ tsp smoked paprika

¼ tsp dried oregano

¼ tsp cayenne, optional

½ tsp salt

1½ cups (360 ml) chicken or vegetable stock

1 tbsp (16 g) tomato paste

To make the enchilada sauce, heat the olive oil in a saucepan over medium heat. Add the flour, whisking constantly for 1 minute.

Add the chili powder, cumin, garlic powder, smoked paprika, oregano, cayenne (if using) and salt. Cook an additional minute, whisking constantly.

Whisk in the chicken or vegetable stock a little at a time. Add the tomato paste and mix until smooth.

Bring the sauce to a simmer then reduce the heat to medium-low and cook for 10 minutes, stirring occasionally. Remove the pan from the heat and set aside.

(continued)

Enchiladas

1 tbsp (15 ml) olive oil

1 yellow onion, chopped

1 poblano pepper, seeds removed and chopped

Salt, to taste

1 (4-oz [113-g]) can diced green chilis

1 tsp ground cumin

2 cloves garlic, minced

1 cup (136 g) sweet corn kernels, fresh or frozen and thawed

1 (15-oz [425-g]) can black beans, drained and rinsed

8 flour tortillas

1 cup (113 g) shredded cheddar cheese

1 cup (113 g) shredded pepper Jack cheese

Optional Toppings

Sliced avocado

Sliced green onions

Sour cream

Lime wedges

Quick Pickled Red Onions (page 110)

To make the enchiladas, preheat the oven to 400°F (200°C) and spray a 9 x 13-inch (23 x 33-cm) baking dish with nonstick spray.

Warm the olive oil in a large skillet over medium heat. Add the onion, poblano pepper and a pinch of salt. Let the vegetables sauté for 4 minutes.

Add the green chilis, cumin and garlic. Let the mixture cook for about 1 minute, stirring frequently. Remove the pan from the heat and add the mixture to a large mixing bowl with the corn and beans.

Assemble the enchiladas by adding a little bit of the vegetable mixture to a tortilla, sprinkling a little of the cheddar cheese on top, rolling it up tightly and placing it in the baking dish folded side down. Repeat with all of the tortillas. If there's leftover mixture, add it to the baking dish.

Pour the enchilada sauce on top and then sprinkle with the shredded pepper Jack cheese. Bake for 18 to 20 minutes.

Serve with your desired toppings.

SHEET-PAN CHICKEN FAJITAS WITH JALAPEÑO SAUCE

Nothing reminds me of a Tex-Mex restaurant more than a sizzling plate of fajitas. I don't think anything turns heads quite like it. These sheet-pan chicken fajitas are so easy to make at home. The jalapeño sauce really ties everything together and gives the dish a unique twist. My husband and I love making a pitcher of margaritas to enjoy with this meal, too!

Yield: 4 servings

Jalapeño Sauce

½ cup (120 ml) sour cream

1 jalapeño, seeds removed for a mild sauce, chopped

¼ cup (4 g) cilantro leaves

2 tbsp (30 ml) lime juice

2 cloves garlic, peeled

½ tsp salt

3 tbsp (40 g) chopped pickled jalapeños

Preheat the oven to 425°F (220°C) and spray a large baking sheet with nonstick cooking spray.

To make the jalapeño sauce, add the sour cream, jalapeño, cilantro leaves, lime juice, garlic and salt to a blender or food processor. Blend until smooth. Taste and add more lime or salt if necessary. Stir in the chopped pickled jalapeños.

Cover the sauce and refrigerate until ready to use.

(continued)

Sheet-Pan Chicken Fajitas

2 tsp (6 g) chipotle chili powder, or regular chili powder

1 tsp ground cumin

1 tsp garlic powder

1 tsp adobo seasoning

½ tsp smoked paprika

¼ tsp dried oregano

1 tsp salt

½ tsp ground black pepper

1½ lb (680 g) chicken breast, boneless and skinless, cut into thin strips against the grain

2 tbsp (30 ml) avocado oil, divided

3 bell peppers, seeds and ribs removed, thinly sliced

1 yellow onion, thinly sliced

8–10 flour tortillas

1 lime

Chopped cilantro, to taste

To make the fajitas, in a small mixing bowl, combine the chipotle chili powder, cumin, garlic powder, adobo seasoning, smoked paprika, dried oregano, salt and pepper. Mix well.

In a large mixing bowl, combine the chicken strips with 1 tablespoon (15 ml) of the avocado oil and almost all of the seasoning blend. Mix well to coat the chicken strips.

In another large mixing bowl, combine the bell peppers and onion with the other tablespoon (15 ml) of avocado oil and the remaining seasoning blend. Mix well.

Place the chicken, bell peppers and onion on the prepared sheet pan. Bake for 20 to 23 minutes.

Wrap the tortillas in foil and place them in the oven to warm for the last 5 minutes of cook time.

Remove the sheet pan from the oven and squeeze the lime over the chicken, bell peppers and onion. Top with the chopped cilantro. Serve with the jalapeño sauce and warmed tortillas.

SHEET-PAN SHRIMP & CHEESY RANCH POTATOES

File this sheet-pan meal under "effortless-yet-delicious dinners." I love combining a southern staple like cheesy ranch potatoes with spicy seasoned shrimp. It's the perfect Texan and Mexican combination made in one easy meal. Plus, you won't have a sink full of dishes when you're done making it!

⇒ *Yield: 4 servings* ⇐

1½ lb (680 g) red potatoes, cut into small pieces

2 tbsp (30 ml) olive oil, divided

2 tbsp (17 g) dry ranch seasoning

1 tsp smoked paprika, divided

Pinch of cayenne

Salt and pepper

1 lb (454 g) shrimp, peeled and deveined, tails on if desired

2 tsp (6 g) chili powder

1 tsp garlic powder

½ cup (57 g) shredded pepper Jack cheese

2 tbsp (2 g) chopped cilantro

Preheat the oven to 400°F (200°C). Line a large baking sheet with foil then spray the foil with nonstick spray.

In a large mixing bowl, combine the potatoes with 1 tablespoon (15 ml) of the olive oil, the ranch seasoning, ½ teaspoon of smoked paprika, cayenne and a generous sprinkle of salt and pepper. Mix well.

Add the potatoes to one side of the prepared baking sheet. Bake for 23 minutes, or until golden and tender.

Meanwhile, in a large mixing bowl, combine the shrimp with the remaining tablespoon (15 ml) of olive oil and the chili powder, garlic powder, ½ teaspoon of smoked paprika, salt and pepper.

Remove the pan from the oven and sprinkle the cheese on the potatoes and add the shrimp to the other side of the baking sheet. Bake for 8 to 10 minutes, or until the shrimp are cooked through.

Top with the chopped cilantro and serve.

SALSA VERDE CHICKEN CASSEROLE

This is not your average casserole. Salsa verde is a great way to add a pop of zesty flavor to any meal. It's got the perfect kick and fresh taste to spice up anything from enchiladas, soups and tacos to, in this case, a casserole! A huge bonus is that this dish makes great leftovers! But I doubt you'll have any.

Yield: 4–6 servings

2½ cups (350 g) shredded cooked chicken

2 cups (480 ml) Tomatillo Salsa Verde (page 106), or 16 oz (454 g) store-bought salsa verde, divided

1 (16-oz [454-g]) can pinto beans, drained and rinsed

1 cup (136 g) corn kernels, fresh or frozen and thawed

1 (4-oz [113-g]) can diced green chilis

1 tsp cumin

½ tsp paprika

¼ tsp cayenne

½ tsp garlic powder

Salt and pepper, to taste

1½ cups (170 g) shredded pepper Jack cheese, divided

4 (8-inch [20-cm]) flour tortillas

Fresh or pickled jalapeños, for topping

1 tbsp (1 g) chopped cilantro, for topping

Avocado slices, for topping, optional

Lime wedges, for topping

Sour cream, for topping, optional

Preheat the oven to 400°F (200°C) and lightly spray a 9 x 13-inch (23 x 33-cm) baking dish with nonstick cooking spray.

In a large mixing bowl, combine the shredded chicken, 1 cup (240 ml) of the salsa verde, the pinto beans, corn, green chilis, cumin, paprika, cayenne, garlic powder, salt and pepper.

Add about half of the chicken mixture to the bottom of the prepared baking dish followed by ½ cup (57 g) of the pepper Jack cheese and two of the tortillas.

Add the rest of the chicken mixture on top of the tortillas and make sure to evenly spread it, followed by ½ cup (57 g) of the pepper Jack cheese and two more tortillas.

Add the remaining 1 cup (240 ml) of salsa verde on top and the final ½ cup (57 g) of pepper Jack cheese.

Cover the dish with foil and bake for 35 minutes, then uncover and bake for 10 more minutes. Let the casserole sit for 5 minutes before slicing and serving.

Top with pickled jalapeños, cilantro and avocado, if using. Serve with lime wedges and sour cream, if using.

FIESTA CASSEROLE

This dish is the ultimate weeknight dinner. Throw everything together and let it bake—it's that easy! Slice it and serve it with your favorite toppings like sour cream, avocado and cilantro. This is another recipe that makes for great leftovers! And you'll definitely look forward to eating these leftovers. Think a big baked taco with the added zing of a rich enchilada sauce. Yum!

Yield: 6 servings

1 lb (454 g) ground beef

Salt and pepper

1 tsp garlic powder

1 tsp ground cumin

1 tsp chili powder

½ tsp paprika

Pinch of cayenne, optional

½ cup (58 g) finely chopped yellow onion

1 jalapeño, seeds removed, finely chopped

1 (15-oz [425-g]) can black beans, drained and rinsed

2 cups (480 ml) store-bought red enchilada sauce or my enchilada sauce (page 67), divided

1½ cups (170 g) shredded Mexican cheese blend, divided

4 (8-inch [20-cm]) flour tortillas

1 tbsp (1 g) chopped cilantro

Lime wedges, for serving

Sour cream, optional

Avocado slices, optional

Preheat the oven to 375°F (190°C) and lightly spray a 9 x 13-inch (23 x 33-cm) baking dish with nonstick cooking spray.

To a large nonstick skillet over medium heat, add the ground beef. Season the meat with a pinch of salt and pepper and cook until it is browned, crumbling it as it cooks, 5 to 7 minutes.

When the ground beef is almost done cooking, add the garlic powder, cumin, chili powder, paprika and cayenne (if using). Toss to evenly coat the beef. Remove the beef from the pan, using a slotted spoon to get rid of some of the grease, and add it to a bowl. Set the bowl aside.

Wipe the pan clean and add the onion and jalapeño. Season with a little salt and pepper. Let it cook for 3 to 4 minutes, stirring frequently. Add the beef back to the skillet, along with the black beans and 1½ cups (360 ml) of the enchilada sauce.

Let the mixture simmer for about 2 minutes, then remove the pan from heat. Add half of the mixture to the bottom of the baking dish followed by ½ cup (57 g) of cheese and two tortillas.

Then add the other half of the beef mixture followed by another ½ cup (57 g) of the cheese, two tortillas, the remaining ½ cup (120 ml) of enchilada sauce and ½ cup (57 g) of cheese. Cover the dish with foil and bake for 30 minutes.

Remove the foil and bake for another 5 to 7 minutes uncovered. Let the casserole rest for at least 3 minutes before slicing into six square servings.

Top with the chopped cilantro and serve with lime wedges, sour cream and avocado slices, if desired.

TACO-STUFFED POBLANO PEPPERS

Craving something healthy but still satisfying? These taco-stuffed poblano peppers are always in rotation at my house. Poblanos have a great fresh taste and go so well with any Tex-Mex–inspired dish. The toppings are very important with this meal. So, don't skimp on them! Smashed Guacamole (page 105), hot sauce and Quick Pickled Red Onions (page 110) are nonnegotiable for me.

⋛ Yield: 4 servings ⋚

4 poblano peppers

1 tbsp (15 ml) olive oil

1 lb (454 g) ground beef

2 tbsp (32 g) tomato paste

1 tbsp (8 g) chili powder

1 tsp ground cumin

½ tsp smoked paprika

1 tsp garlic powder

½ tsp onion powder

⅛ tsp cayenne

Salt, to taste

1 (15-oz [425-g]) can black beans, drained and rinsed

1 cup (113 g) shredded Monterey Jack cheese

Pico de Gallo (page 109), for topping

Smashed Guacamole (page 105), for topping

Quick Pickled Red Onions (page 110), for topping

Hot sauce, for topping

Chopped cilantro, for topping

Preheat the oven to 350°F (175°C).

Slice each poblano in half lengthwise. Remove the seeds and place the peppers in a 9 x 13-inch (23 x 33-cm) baking dish.

Add the olive oil to a skillet over medium heat. Add the beef and break it up until it is cooked through, browned and in small crumbles, about 7 minutes.

Add the tomato paste, chili powder, cumin, smoked paprika, garlic powder, onion powder, cayenne and salt to the skillet. Stir until combined, then stir in the beans.

Divide the cooked beef and bean mixture evenly among the pepper halves. Cover the baking dish in foil and bake for 35 minutes or until the peppers are tender.

Sprinkle the cheese on top and bake the peppers uncovered for 4 to 5 more minutes or until the cheese is melted.

Top with the Pico de Gallo, Smashed Guacamole, Quick Pickled Red Onions, a drizzle of hot sauce and cilantro.

BAKED SALMON WITH AVOCADO SALSA

This healthy meal has a wonderful little Tex-Mex spin on it. It's seasoned with hot and smoky spices then baked to perfection. The avocado salsa adds such a fresh touch. In Texas I've learned that salsas of any kind can really take a dish to the next level. This dinner is colorful, nourishing and packed with flavor. It is my favorite way to eat salmon!

Yield: 4 servings

Avocado Salsa

2 ripe avocados, pitted and diced

1 tbsp (15 ml) lime juice

1 tbsp (1 g) fresh cilantro, chopped

1 Roma tomato, chopped

1 small jalapeño, seeded and finely chopped

Salt, to taste

Baked Salmon

2 tbsp (28 g) brown sugar

½ tsp smoked paprika

1 tsp ground cumin

1 tsp chili powder

¼ tsp garlic powder

Salt, to taste

4 salmon fillets

1 tbsp (15 ml) olive oil

In a small mixing bowl, combine the avocado, lime juice, cilantro, tomato, jalapeño and salt. Cover and refrigerate until ready to use.

Preheat the oven to 400°F (200°C) and line a baking sheet with foil.

In a small mixing bowl, combine the brown sugar, smoked paprika, cumin, chili powder, garlic powder and salt.

Lay the salmon fillets on the baking sheet, skin side down. Brush the olive oil on the salmon fillets then coat them with the seasoning mixture.

Bake the salmon for 12 to 13 minutes, or until the salmon is flaky and cooked through. Serve each fillet topped with the avocado salsa.

CROWD-PLEASING APPETIZERS

Dips, finger food, nachos . . . these are a few of my favorite things. There's nothing I love more than a gathering where everyone brings their own appetizer. Then it's just a spread of various snacks. It's the little things in life.

I hope you find something in here that you can bring to get-togethers time and time again, because everyone loved it so much. Whether it's for a tailgate, holiday party or margarita night with friends, there is something in this chapter for every occasion.

In this chapter, you can find some Tex-Mex classics like queso (page 96) and Cowboy Caviar (page 99), which is a must-have at any Texas gathering. Then there's the Street Corn Sheet-Pan Nachos (page 84), Pimento Cheese Corn Dip (page 92) and a handful of other fun and unique recipes that will highlight the best of Tex-Mex cuisine!

STREET CORN SHEET-PAN NACHOS

For this party appetizer, I combined two of my favorite Mexican dishes: Mexican street corn *(elote)* and nachos! It's beyond easy to make and even easier to eat. I love topping this with my homemade Pico de Gallo (page 109), Quick Pickled Red Onions (page 110) and cilantro. Pro tip: Sturdy tortilla chips do best for this recipe.

⋛ *Yield: 4–6 servings* ⋚

1 large bag tortilla chips, about 8 oz (226 g)

1 (15-oz [425-g]) can corn kernels, drained

1 lime, juiced

3 tbsp (45 ml) sour cream

2 tbsp (30 ml) mayonnaise

1 tsp chili powder, plus more for topping

¼ tsp garlic powder

½ tsp smoked paprika

Pinch of cayenne

Salt and pepper, to taste

1½ cups (170 g) shredded Mexican cheese

3 tbsp (24 g) crumbled cotija cheese

Pico de Gallo (page 109)

Quick Pickled Red Onions (page 110)

1 tbsp (1 g) chopped cilantro

Preheat the oven to 400°F (200°C) and line a large baking sheet with foil for easy cleanup.

Spread the tortilla chips on the prepared baking sheet.

To a small mixing bowl, add the corn, lime juice, sour cream, mayo, chili powder, garlic powder, smoked paprika, cayenne, salt and pepper. Mix to combine. Evenly spread the corn mix on top of the tortilla chips.

Sprinkle the shredded Mexican cheese on top of the corn mixture and add a pinch more chili powder on top of the nachos. Bake for about 10 minutes, until the cheese is melted and gooey.

Top with the cotija cheese, Pico de Gallo, pickled red onions and cilantro.

Serve immediately and enjoy!

TEXAS-STYLE NACHOS

The true Texas-style nacho is a singular tortilla chip with refried beans, melted cheese and a pickled jalapeño on top. Bake a whole bunch of these and serve them for a fun appetizer. The best part is every chip has equal amounts of toppings so no one is missing out on the flavor! I like drizzling mine with some hot sauce. My personal favorite hot sauces are Valentina, Cholula and Frank's RedHot.

Yield: 20 nachos

20 tortilla chips

1 cup (230 g) refried beans

1 cup (113 g) shredded Colby Jack cheese, or shredded cheese of choice

20 pickled jalapeños

Hot sauce

1 tbsp (1 g) chopped cilantro

Preheat the oven to 400°F (200°C) and line a large baking sheet with foil or spray the sheet with nonstick cooking spray.

Arrange the tortilla chips in a single layer on the baking sheet. Top each tortilla chip with a spoonful of refried beans followed by a sprinkle of cheese. Place one pickled jalapeño on each chip.

Bake the nachos for 8 to 10 minutes.

Drizzle the chips with hot sauce and chopped cilantro. Crack open your favorite beer and enjoy!

MINI JALAPEÑO CRAB CAKES WITH LEMON AIOLI

I absolutely love a good crab cake. These bite-sized ones are so much fun to serve at a get-together. I guarantee they will be gone in minutes. The jalapeño gives a little kick of Tex-Mex and the lemon aioli is the perfect rich and creamy dipping sauce.

Yield: 12 crab cakes

Lemon Aioli

¾ cup (180 ml) mayonnaise

1 tbsp (15 ml) lemon juice

½ tsp lemon zest

1 tsp Dijon mustard

½ tsp garlic powder

Salt and pepper, to taste

Crab Cakes

1 lb (454 g) lump crab meat

¼ cup (60 ml) mayonnaise

1 egg, whisked

1 tsp hot sauce

1 cup (56 g) panko breadcrumbs, divided

1 jalapeño, seeds removed and finely diced

½ tsp Old Bay seasoning

Salt and pepper

2 tbsp (30 ml) olive oil

1 tbsp (4 g) chopped parsley leaves, optional

Lemon wedges, for topping

Lemon zest, for topping

To make the lemon aioli, combine the mayonnaise, lemon juice, lemon zest, Dijon mustard, garlic powder, salt and pepper in a small mixing bowl. Cover and refrigerate until ready to use.

To make the crab cakes, in a medium mixing bowl, combine the crab meat with the mayonnaise, egg, hot sauce, ¾ cup (42 g) of the panko breadcrumbs, jalapeño, Old Bay seasoning and a pinch of salt and pepper. Mix well.

Shape the mixture into 12 small crab cakes. Lightly coat each one in the remaining panko breadcrumbs. Place the mini crab cakes in the refrigerator for 30 minutes to set.

Heat the olive oil in a large skillet over medium heat. When heated, add the crab cakes and cook for 3 to 4 minutes per side, or until golden.

Top with the chopped parsley, lemon wedges and lemon zest, if desired, and serve with the lemon aioli.

SWEET & SPICY BBQ SLIDERS

Sliders are a go-to recipe for me when it comes to gatherings, game days or holiday parties. They're such a fun finger food that people always seem to love. These sweet and spicy sliders have layers of flavor. There's subtle sweetness from the Hawaiian rolls, peach preserves and honey. Then there's bold spice from the pickled jalapeños and pepper Jack cheese. Each bite tastes simply amazing.

⋛ Yield: 12 sliders ⋚

1 (12-oz [340-g]) package of Hawaiian sweet slider rolls, split

2½ cups (350 g) cooked shredded chicken or Pellet Grill Pulled Pork (page 60)

¾ cup (180 ml) Easy Homemade BBQ Sauce (page 113)

¼ cup (80 g) peach preserves

12–16 pickled jalapeños, plus more, for topping

1½ cups (170 g) shredded pepper Jack cheese

2 tbsp (30 ml) melted butter

1 tbsp (15 ml) honey

Preheat the oven to 350°F (175°C). Arrange the bottom half of the slider rolls in a 9 x 13-inch (23 x 30-cm) baking dish.

In a large mixing bowl, combine the shredded chicken or pulled pork, barbecue sauce and peach preserves. Mix to combine.

Evenly spoon the peach barbecue chicken or pork on top of each roll, followed by the pickled jalapeños and shredded pepper Jack.

In a small bowl, stir the melted butter and honey to combine.

Place the top half of the rolls on top of the filling, then brush the melted butter and honey on top of each roll.

Cover the dish with foil and bake for 20 minutes. Then, uncover and bake an additional 8 minutes, or until the sliders are golden. Place some pickled jalapeños on top and enjoy!

PIMENTO CHEESE CORN DIP

A good dip recipe is my weakness. Especially when it's as cheesy as this one!
This hot pimento cheese corn dip is guaranteed to be a crowd pleaser. It's one of those
things that you can't stop eating once you start because it's that delicious. Pimento cheese
is a southern staple. I added a little Tex-Mex twist by adding corn and some spice. Serve it
with tortilla chips or some crackers at a gathering and I'm sure people will
be begging you for the recipe.

Yield: 8–10 servings

8 oz (226 g) cream cheese, softened

⅓ cup (80 ml) mayonnaise

2 tsp (12 ml) hot sauce

1 tsp ground mustard

1 tsp smoked paprika

1 tsp ground cumin

Salt and pepper, to taste

8 oz (226 g) shredded sharp cheddar cheese

1 (4-oz [113-g]) can diced pimentos, drained

2 cups (272 g) sweet corn kernels, fresh or frozen and thawed

Sliced green onion for topping, optional

Tortilla chips or crackers, for serving

Preheat the oven to 375°F (190°C).

In a large mixing bowl, combine the cream cheese, mayo, hot sauce, ground mustard, smoked paprika, cumin, salt and pepper. Mix well to combine.

Mix in the shredded cheddar cheese, pimentos and corn. Add the mixture to an 8 x 8-inch (20 x 20–cm) baking dish and bake for 25 to 28 minutes or until bubbly and hot.

Top with sliced green onion (if using) and serve with tortilla chips or crackers.

BAKED BEAN DIP

This dish is also known as "Texas trash dip." Whatever you want to call it, it's always delicious! The combo of spicy baked refried beans topped with melty cheese is to die for. This appetizer is perfect for a get-together, game day or just a midday snack. It makes a lot but also is great reheated the next day.

⋛ *Yield: 12–15 servings* ⋚

8 oz (226 g) cream cheese, softened

½ cup (120 ml) sour cream

2 (16-oz [454-g]) cans refried beans

1 tbsp (8 g) chili powder

1 tbsp (6 g) ground cumin

1 tsp garlic powder

Salt, to taste

½ cup (135 g) pickled jalapeños, chopped

1½ cups (170 g) shredded pepper Jack cheese

¼ cup (32 g) black olive slices

1 tbsp (3 g) sliced green onion

Tortillas chips, for serving

Preheat the oven to 350°F (175°C).

In a large mixing bowl, combine the cream cheese and sour cream, mixing until smooth.

Add the refried beans, chili powder, cumin, garlic powder, salt and chopped pickled jalapenos. Mix well.

Spread the mixture into an 8 x 12–inch (20 x 30–cm) baking dish. Top the dip with the shredded pepper Jack cheese and bake for 25 to 30 minutes.

Take the dip out of the oven and top with the sliced black olives and sliced green onion. Serve with tortilla chips on the side.

CREAMY QUESO

I didn't know good queso until I moved to Texas. Let me tell you, I was surely missing out. It's a big deal in the Lone Star State and Tex-Mex cuisine. Every Tex-Mex restaurant has a version of it on their menu. Serve it with chips, on top of nachos, tacos, burritos . . . it will be good on almost anything in this book. You can't go wrong with a big bowl of melty, salty cheese spiced just right.

Yield: 5–6 servings

1 tbsp (14 g) butter

⅓ cup (53 g) chopped yellow onion

1 jalapeño, seeded and finely chopped

1 (4-oz [113-g]) can diced green chilis

½ tsp ground cumin

1 tsp chipotle chili powder, or chili powder

Salt, to taste

2 cloves garlic, minced

1 lb (454 g) American cheese, cubed

2 oz (57 g) cream cheese, at room temperature

1½ cups (360 ml) half and half

1 cup (113 g) shredded cheddar cheese

Chopped cilantro, for topping

Jalapeño slices, for topping

A drizzle of hot sauce (I like Valentina's for this recipe)

Tortilla chips, for serving

In a skillet over medium heat, melt the butter. When melted, add the onion, jalapeño, diced green chilis, cumin, chipotle chili powder and salt.

Cook for 5 to 7 minutes, stirring occasionally. Add the garlic and let cook for 30 seconds.

Add the cubed American cheese, cream cheese and half and half. Mix and let cook until it's smooth and creamy; this should only take a minute or so.

Stir in the shredded cheddar cheese and mix to combine. Keep whisking the queso until the consistency becomes smooth and creamy, 3 to 5 minutes. Taste and adjust seasonings if need be. If you want a "looser" queso, you can whisk in a little more half and half or water.

Ladle the queso into a serving bowl and top with the chopped cilantro, jalapeño slices and a drizzle of hot sauce. Serve with chips.

COWBOY CAVIAR

Fresh cowboy caviar is a Texas staple. It's a cold bean salad that's perfect for dipping tortilla chips in. Everyone makes it a little differently. Some like using black-eyed peas, but I prefer the combination of black beans, pinto beans and corn. It sure gets hot in Texas so the more "no-cook" recipes, the better!

Yield: 6 servings

1 (15-oz [425-g]) can black beans, drained and rinsed

1 (15-oz [425-g]) can pinto beans, drained and rinsed

1 cup (136 g) corn kernels, fresh or frozen and thawed

1 cup (180 g) chopped tomatoes

½ medium red onion, finely chopped

1 jalapeño, seeds removed, finely chopped

¼ cup (4 g) chopped cilantro

1 chipotle in adobo sauce, finely chopped

1 tbsp (15 ml) adobo sauce

Juice of 2 limes

1 tbsp (15 ml) olive oil

1 tbsp (15 ml) honey

1 tsp chili powder

1 tsp ground cumin

1 tsp salt

In a large mixing bowl, combine the black beans, pinto beans, corn, tomatoes, red onion, jalapeño and cilantro.

In a small mixing bowl, whisk together the chipotle, adobo sauce, lime juice, olive oil, honey, chili powder, cumin and salt. Then pour over the bean mixture. Toss to combine.

Cover and refrigerate your cowboy caviar or serve immediately.

THE BEST SALSAS & FIXINS

At just about any Tex-Mex restaurant, you'll be seated, then immediately greeted with chips and salsa. It's the bread and butter of this cuisine. Not only is it a fantastic starter to share amongst friends and family, but salsa is also an important topping. Pico de Gallo (page 109) adds the perfect touch to any taco, burrito or enchilada, or almost any recipe in this book for that matter!

Another big component of Tex-Mex food is guacamole (page 105). Guacamole might just be one of my favorite things in the world. Luckily, in Texas it's made a variety of ways and is always so fresh and satisfying.

In this chapter, you can find a handful of other salsas and toppings that add a little something extra to any dish!

MANGO OR PINEAPPLE SALSA

There are a ton of different ways to use a good fruit salsa. Throw it on tacos, over grilled chicken or fish, serve it with tortilla chips or add it to a rice bowl. It adds such a summery feel to any recipe. I love the pineapple version on my Grilled Chicken Street Tacos (page 17) and mango salsa is my favorite on top of lighter dishes like baked salmon.

Yield: 2½ cups (620 g)

2 cups (500 g) chopped mango or pineapple

1 jalapeño, seeds removed, finely diced

1 red bell pepper, seeds and ribs removed, finely chopped

¼ cup (4 g) cilantro, chopped

¼ cup (40 g) finely chopped red onion, optional

Juice of ½ lime

Salt, to taste

In a medium mixing bowl, combine the mango or pineapple with the jalapeño, red bell pepper, cilantro, red onion (if using), lime juice and salt.

Cover and refrigerate until ready to use. Serve on its own with tortilla chips or accompanying your favorite taco or quesadilla!

This will last in a container in the refrigerator for 2 to 3 days.

SMASHED GUACAMOLE

What would a Tex-Mex cookbook be without a guacamole recipe? I know guacamole is simple, but it's one of the best foods. Bring me a margarita, guacamole and chips and I am one happy girl. The cool thing about guacamole is that everyone does it a little differently. I like mine smashed (leaving some of that avocado texture in there) with creamy crumbled cotija cheese and nutty pepitas, with a whole lot of salty tortilla chips.

Yield: 4 servings

2 ripe avocados, cut in half, pit removed

1 tbsp (15 ml) lime juice

¼ cup (40 g) chopped red onion

2 Roma tomatoes, chopped

3 tbsp (3 g) cilantro, chopped

Pinch of garlic powder

Salt and pepper, to taste

3 tbsp (24 g) crumbled cotija cheese

2 tbsp (18 g) pepitas or pumpkin seeds

Tortilla chips, for serving

Spoon the avocado into a bowl. Add the lime juice and smash the avocado until it is mostly smooth but with some chunks left.

Add the onion, tomatoes, cilantro, garlic powder, salt and pepper. Mix well to combine. Taste and add more salt, pepper or garlic powder if necessary.

Top the smashed guacamole with the crumbled cotija and pepitas or pumpkin seeds. Serve with a big mound of tortilla chips for dipping.

TOMATILLO SALSA VERDE

This is a simple recipe that goes such a long way. Salsa verde is the foundation of so many recipes in this book. You can buy it premade at just about any grocery store. However, fresh and homemade salsa verde is what I prefer. It's not only easy to throw together, but you can make it as flavorful and spicy as you please. Leave the seeds in the jalapeño if you want it more spicy!

Yield: About 3½ cups (910 g)

1 lb (454 g) tomatillos, husks removed and quartered

2 poblano peppers, seeds removed and cut in half

1 jalapeño, seeds removed and cut in half

1 small yellow onion, skin removed and cut into 5–6 wedges

2–3 cloves garlic, peeled

1 tbsp (15 ml) lime juice

½ cup (8 g) fresh cilantro leaves

1 tsp salt

Heat the broiler to high.

Line a large baking sheet with foil and add the tomatillos, poblano peppers, jalapeño and onion. Broil the vegetables on the middle rack for about 10 minutes or until the skin of the peppers is blistered.

Add the roasted tomatillos, poblano peppers, jalapeño and onion to a food processor or high-speed blender. Add the garlic, lime juice, cilantro and salt to the blender. Blend until smooth.

Store the salsa verde in an airtight container or jar with a lid in the refrigerator until ready to use. Serve within 5 to 6 days.

PICO DE GALLO & HOMEMADE CHILI-LIME TORTILLA CHIPS

Pico de gallo is so simple to make and is such a must for many Tex-Mex recipes. Add a little bit over tacos or nachos for additional fresh flavor, or just enjoy it with some salty tortilla chips. I provided a homemade tortilla chip recipe for you to try out with a chili-lime seasoning—you can use it for any of the recipes in this book that call for tortilla chips if you want! Homemade tortilla chips are surprisingly quick and easy to make yourself. If you like a spicier pico de gallo, leave the seeds in your jalapeño for some heat.

Yield: 3½ cups (840 g) pico de gallo and about 24 chips

Pico de Gallo

2½ cups (450 g) diced Roma tomatoes

1 jalapeño, seeded and finely diced

¼ cup (40 g) finely chopped red onion

¼ cup (4 g) cilantro leaves, chopped

½ tsp salt

Juice of ½ a lime

Tortilla Chips

½ tbsp (8 ml) olive oil

Salt, to taste

¼ tsp chili powder

½ tsp lime juice

6 corn tortillas

In a mixing bowl, combine the tomatoes, jalapeño, red onion, cilantro, salt and lime juice. Mix well. Store in the fridge until ready to serve.

To make the tortilla chips, preheat the oven to 350°F (175°C). In a small mixing bowl, combine the olive oil, salt, chili powder and lime juice.

Cut the corn tortillas into four to six triangles then brush the oil mixture on each side of the chips. Place them on a large baking sheet in a single layer.

Bake the chips for 15 to 20 minutes, or until crispy and golden.

Serve the pico immediately with the chips or store it in an airtight container in the refrigerator until ready to use. Pico de gallo will stay good for up to 3 days in the refrigerator. Chips are best the same day, but store leftovers in a paper bag or airtight container.

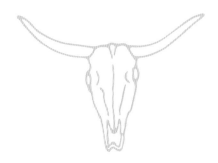

QUICK PICKLED RED ONIONS

Pickled red onions may seem so simple; however, they are the perfect touch to so many recipes in this book. You can throw them on tacos, burrito bowls, salads, enchiladas or nachos. A Mason jar full of these is a refrigerator staple in my home.

Yield: 8 servings

1 red onion, peeled and thinly sliced

¾ cup (180 ml) apple cider vinegar

1 tsp salt

1 tbsp (15 ml) honey

1 tsp peppercorns

Juice of ½ lime

Place the onion slices in an airtight jar, such as a Mason jar.

In a small saucepan over medium-high heat, combine the apple cider vinegar, salt and honey.

Bring the liquid to a simmer then quickly pour the mixture into the jar with the onions. Add the peppercorns and lime juice.

Cover the jar with its lid and let the onions marinate in the refrigerator for at least 30 minutes before using. Store in a sealed container in the refrigerator for up to 10 days.

EASY HOMEMADE BBQ SAUCE

I know barbecue sauce can be found at any grocery store. However, it's actually insanely easy to make at home. This Texas-style–inspired BBQ sauce recipe is great for drizzling on smoked brisket (page 59), smothering on chicken wings (pages 48 and 51) or adding to a pulled pork sandwich (page 60). I make mine with canned tomato sauce, but if you want a thicker sauce, you can use ketchup instead.

⸞ *Yield: 2 cups (480 ml)* ⸟

1 (15-oz [425-g]) can tomato sauce

¼ cup + 1 tbsp (69 g) brown sugar

¼ cup (60 ml) apple cider vinegar

¼ cup (60 ml) molasses

1 tsp liquid smoke

2 tbsp (30 ml) Worcestershire sauce

1 tsp onion powder

1 tsp garlic powder

1 tsp ground mustard

½ tsp smoked paprika

¼ tsp cayenne

1 tsp salt

In a small or medium saucepan, combine the tomato sauce, brown sugar, apple cider vinegar, molasses, liquid smoke, Worcestershire sauce, onion powder, garlic powder, ground mustard, smoked paprika, cayenne and salt and place it over low heat.

Simmer the sauce for 15 to 20 minutes, stirring frequently.

Taste the sauce and adjust any seasonings if necessary.

Let the BBQ sauce cool and serve immediately or store it in an airtight container in the refrigerator for up to 2 weeks.

SERIOUSLY GOOD
SIDES

Side dishes are a huge part of any meal, especially when they're as delicious as the ones in this chapter! Tex-Mex sides are far from boring. Some of the recipes in this chapter would be perfect with a hearty BBQ meal, like my Pickleback Slaw (page 119) or Slow Cooker Ranch-Style Beans (page 123), while others complement a taco spread, such as Tex-Mex Fried Rice (page 124) and smoky Chipotle Slaw (page 116).

Then, of course, there should always be a veggie! I love taking simple vegetables and turning them into something drool-worthy—like my Hot Honey Brussels Sprouts (page 128) or vibrant Southwest Wedge Salad (page 120).

Side dishes are often looked past even though they're such a big component of a balanced meal. Thankfully, all of the sides in this chapter are super easy to make and even easier to eat!

CHIPOTLE SLAW

This is not your average coleslaw. The smoky chipotle flavors make this slaw a great option on tacos! My Blackened Fish Tacos (page 13) and this slaw are a match made in heaven. You can also serve this slaw as a BBQ side with some of Robbie's Smoked Brisket (page 59) and Pellet Grill Pulled Pork (page 60).

⋛ *Yield: 6 servings* ⋚

½ cup (120 ml) mayonnaise

1 chipotle pepper in adobo sauce

2 tbsp (30 ml) adobo sauce

2 tsp (10 ml) apple cider vinegar

6 cups (420 g) shredded cabbage, purple and green

1 tbsp (15 g) granulated sugar

1 tsp ground cumin

½ tsp paprika

¼ tsp garlic powder

1 tsp salt

½ tsp ground black pepper

In a food processor or blender, blend the mayonnaise, chipotle pepper, adobo sauce and apple cider vinegar until smooth.

In a large mixing bowl, combine the shredded cabbage, chipotle mayonnaise mixture, sugar, cumin, paprika, garlic powder, salt and pepper.

Taste the slaw and adjust the seasonings if necessary. Cover and refrigerate until ready to serve. Give the slaw a quick toss before serving. This slaw stays good for up to 2 to 3 days in the fridge.

PICKLEBACK SLAW

If you're a pickle lover, this slaw was made for you. Serve it on some burgers or my Chopped Brisket Tacos (page 18). Honestly, I can just eat it by the spoonful because it's that good. It's creamy, tangy and straight-up delicious, which makes it the ideal southern side dish.

Yield: 6 servings

6 cups (420 g) shredded cabbage, green and purple

1 cup (45 g) shredded carrots

½ cup (120 ml) mayonnaise

3 tbsp (45 ml) pickle juice

2 tbsp (30 g) dill pickle relish

½ tbsp (8 ml) Dijon mustard

¼ tsp cayenne

¼ tsp garlic powder

Salt and pepper, to taste

In a large mixing bowl, combine the cabbage and carrots.

In a separate mixing bowl, combine the mayonnaise, pickle juice, dill pickle relish, Dijon mustard, cayenne, garlic powder, salt and pepper.

Pour the mayonnaise mixture over the cabbage and carrots and mix to combine. Taste the slaw and adjust any seasonings if needed.

Cover the slaw and refrigerate until ready to use. Give the slaw a quick toss before serving. This slaw stays good for up to 2 to 3 days in the fridge.

SOUTHWEST WEDGE SALAD

This recipe puts a little southwest twist on the classic wedge salad: crispy iceberg lettuce with all the fixins on top! The chipotle ranch dressing is creamy, tangy and smoky. I suggest doubling or tripling the dressing recipe so you can save some in the fridge for future salads!

Yield: 4–6 servings

Chipotle Ranch Dressing

¾ cup (180 ml) sour cream

1 tsp apple cider vinegar

1 tbsp (8 g) dry ranch seasoning

1 chipotle in adobo sauce

1 tbsp (15 ml) adobo sauce

1 tbsp (15 ml) olive oil

Pinch of salt

Wedge Salad

1 head of iceberg lettuce, cut into 4–6 wedges

½ cup (68 g) corn kernels

½ cup (80 g) cherry tomatoes, halved

¼ cup (30 g) crumbled queso fresco cheese

2 tbsp (2 g) cilantro leaves, chopped

¼ cup (14 g) tortilla strips

Fresh cracked black pepper, to taste

To make the dressing, add the sour cream, apple cider vinegar, ranch seasoning, chipotle, adobo sauce, olive oil and salt to a food processor or blender. Blend until smooth. Taste the dressing and adjust any seasonings if necessary. Store in a small bottle or Mason jar in the refrigerator until ready to use. The dressing can be stored in the refrigerator for up to 1 week.

Assemble the wedge salads by placing one wedge of iceberg lettuce on each plate. Evenly divide the corn, cherry tomatoes, queso fresco, cilantro and tortilla strips on top of each wedge.

Add your desired amount of chipotle ranch dressing and fresh black pepper to taste to each wedge. Serve immediately.

SLOW COOKER RANCH-STYLE BEANS

These ranch-style beans are the perfect Tex-Mex side. They do a great job of balancing out both sides of the cuisine. These beans go great with BBQ like smoked brisket (page 59) or with nearly any plate of tacos in this book. They're a southwestern classic and made so easily in a slow cooker. I love topping mine with some shredded sharp cheddar cheese and chopped cilantro.

⋛ *Yield: 6 servings* ⋚

1 (16-oz [454-g]) package of dried pinto beans, rinsed well

¼ cup (66 g) tomato paste

1 tsp apple cider vinegar

1 small yellow onion, finely chopped

2 cloves garlic, minced

1 tbsp (6 g) ground cumin

2 tsp (6 g) chili powder

1 tbsp (14 g) brown sugar

1 tsp salt

½ tsp ground black pepper

7 cups (1.7 L) water

Shredded cheddar cheese, for topping, optional

Chopped cilantro, for topping, optional

Add the beans, tomato paste, apple cider vinegar, onion, garlic, cumin, chili powder, brown sugar, salt, pepper and water to a slow cooker.

Cover and cook the beans on low for 8 hours. By the end of the 8 hours the beans should be soft and stew-like and smell deliciously rich.

Top with shredded cheddar cheese and chopped cilantro, if desired. Serve these beans up in a bowl, or right alongside a plate of tacos or BBQ.

TEX-MEX FRIED RICE

This fried rice belongs on every Taco Tuesday menu. The jalapeño, chipotle chili powder and salsa give it some Tex-Mex style. It has just the right amount of spice and is incredibly easy to whip up. You can even use your leftover rice from take-out for this! It's simple but has a restaurant-quality side dish taste.

⸔ *Yield: 4 servings* ⸕

3 tbsp (45 ml) olive oil, divided

½ cup (80 g) finely chopped yellow onion

1 jalapeño, seeds removed and finely chopped

1 tsp chipotle chili powder or regular chili powder

½ tsp paprika

Pinch of cayenne

½ tsp salt

Pinch of ground black pepper

1 clove garlic, minced

3 cups (560 g) cooked white rice

¼ cup (65 g) premade salsa

Juice of ½ lime

1 tbsp (3 g) sliced green onion

Lime wedges, for serving

Add 1 tablespoon (15 ml) of the olive oil to a large skillet over medium heat.

Add the onion and jalapeño and sauté for 3 minutes. Add the chili powder, paprika, cayenne, salt, pepper and garlic and let the veggies cook for 1 more minute.

Add the remaining 2 tablespoons (30 ml) of the olive oil to the skillet along with the rice and salsa. Cook the rice for 5 minutes, stirring occasionally.

Squeeze in the lime juice and top with sliced green onion. Serve with lime wedges and enjoy.

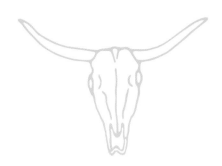

OVEN FRIES WITH PICKLED JALAPEÑO SAUCE

When in doubt for a side dish, fries are always the answer. These oven fries are extremely easy. The key to getting them nice and crispy is to soak the sliced potatoes in cold water before you cook them! I learned this from working in a restaurant and it really does make a difference. Every good fry recipe needs a dipping sauce to go with it. This Tex-Mex–inspired pickled jalapeño sauce will make these fries even more addicting than they already are!

Yield: 4 servings

Oven Fries

2 large russet potatoes

2 tbsp (30 ml) avocado oil

½ tsp paprika

¼ tsp garlic powder

¼ tsp onion powder

Pinch of cayenne

1 tsp salt

1 tsp pepper

Pickled Jalapeño Sauce

⅓ cup (80 ml) mayonnaise

1 tbsp (15 ml) sour cream

1 tbsp (15 g) chopped pickled jalapeños

1 tbsp (15 ml) liquid from the pickled jalapeño jar

½ tsp paprika

½ tsp ground cumin

¼ tsp garlic powder

⅛ tsp onion powder

Salt, to taste

To make the fries, peel the potatoes and cut them into ¼-inch (6-mm) matchsticks.

Fill a large bowl with cold water and add the fries. Let them soak for 30 minutes or up to 1 hour to help remove some of the starch—this will make them extra crispy.

Preheat the oven to 425°F (220°C) and line a baking sheet with parchment paper.

While the fries are soaking, make the pickled jalapeño sauce by combining the mayonnaise, sour cream, chopped pickled jalapeños, pickled jalapeño liquid, paprika, ground cumin, garlic powder, onion powder and salt in a small mixing bowl. Taste and adjust the seasonings if necessary. Cover and refrigerate the sauce until ready to use.

Drain the fries and pat them dry. Add them back to a large mixing bowl along with the avocado oil, paprika, garlic powder, onion powder, cayenne, salt and pepper. Toss the fries to coat them.

Add the fries to the prepared baking sheet in a single layer. Bake them for 40 minutes, or until they are golden and crispy on the outside. Carefully flip the fries halfway through the cooking time.

Serve the fries warm with the pickled jalapeño sauce on the side for dipping.

HOT HONEY BRUSSELS SPROUTS

Brussels sprouts are my all-time favorite veggie. The crispier the better, in my opinion. I'm always looking for different ways to make them. I had Brussels sprouts with hot honey at a restaurant in Texas and I tried to replicate it as soon as I could. The spice from the hot sauce paired with the sweet honey and creamy queso fresco makes this the perfect Tex-Mex side dish.

Yield: 2–3 servings

1 tbsp (15 ml) olive oil

1 lb (454 g) Brussels sprouts, trimmed and halved

Salt and pepper, to taste

Pinch of red pepper flakes, optional

2 tbsp (30 ml) honey

2 tsp (10 ml) hot sauce

1 tsp red wine vinegar

¼ cup (30 g) crumbled queso fresco cheese

Preheat the oven to 400°F (200°C).

Heat the olive oil in an oven-safe skillet or cast-iron skillet over medium-high heat and place the Brussels sprouts cut side down in the skillet. Let them cook for 5 to 7 minutes. Do not stir the Brussels sprouts during this cooking time; you want the bottom sides to be charred.

When the Brussels sprouts are very well done, flip them with tongs, season with salt, pepper and red pepper flakes, if using, then transfer the skillet to the oven and bake for 5 minutes.

While the Brussels sprouts are in the oven, in a small mixing bowl, combine the honey, hot sauce and red wine vinegar.

Carefully remove the skillet from the oven and toss the Brussels sprouts in the hot honey sauce then bake for an additional 3 to 4 minutes.

Remove the skillet from the oven and top the Brussels sprouts with the queso fresco.

SUGAR & BOOZE
A SOUTHERN SEND-OFF

This chapter is all about the final course, dessert. Whether that be a yummy cocktail or a slice of pie is up to you. Good thing you can find both in this chapter!

I've had the best margaritas in my life living in Texas. Honestly, I don't think I've ever had a bad one since living here. Over the years I've mastered making margaritas at home. I love how you can customize them so many different ways: spicy, frozen, fruity, salt rim, chili lime rim. The options are really endless. This chapter has a few of my favorites!

And, of course, don't forget dessert. When it comes to sweets, I like to keep it simple and easy. If I can make it, you can make it. The Cowboy Cookie Skillet on page 135 is hands down my favorite.

CHURRO CHOCOLATE BANANA BREAD

Baking a banana bread is so therapeutic for me. I love making banana bread a bunch of different ways, but I have to say this churro-inspired version is an absolute favorite. Between the cinnamon brown sugar coating and melty chocolate chips, I have to refrain from eating the whole loaf in one day.

⋝ Yield: 1 loaf ⋜

3 ripe bananas

¾ cup (180 ml) honey

4 tbsp (56 g) butter, softened

1 tsp vanilla

2 eggs

2 cups (250 g) all-purpose flour

2 tsp (6 g) cinnamon, divided

1 tsp baking soda

½ tsp salt

½ cup (84 g) dark chocolate chips

1 tbsp (14 g) brown sugar

Preheat the oven to 350°F (175°C) and spray a loaf pan with nonstick spray.

In a stand mixer or blender, mash the ripe bananas until they are smooth and creamy. Add the honey, butter and vanilla to the mixer and mix on medium speed to blend. Whisk in the eggs.

Add the flour, 1 teaspoon of the cinnamon, the baking soda and salt. Mix by hand or with a stand mixer set on medium speed until combined.

Fold in the chocolate chips and pour the batter into the loaf pan.

To make the cinnamon sugar topping, in a small mixing bowl, combine the brown sugar and remaining teaspoon of the cinnamon. Evenly sprinkle the mixture over the banana bread batter.

Bake the banana bread for 50 to 55 minutes, or until golden on the top and a toothpick inserted in the center comes out with only a few crumbs.

Let the bread cool completely in the pan before slicing.

COWBOY COOKIE SKILLET

Texas introduced me to the cowboy cookie and I've been craving them regularly ever since. This is my take on a cowboy cookie in skillet form: chopped pecans, chocolate chips and butterscotch morsels in one gooey cookie skillet. No cast-iron skillet? No problem, just bake it in a square baking pan instead. I strongly suggest serving it with a few scoops of vanilla ice cream. Nothing beats a warm and cold dessert combo.

⌇ *Yield: 6 servings* ⌇

1 cup (227 g) unsalted butter, softened, plus more for greasing the pan

¾ cup (165 g) brown sugar

⅓ cup (66 g) granulated sugar

1 egg, at room temperature

2 tsp (10 ml) vanilla extract

1½ cups (188 g) all-purpose flour

¼ tsp salt

1 tsp ground cinnamon

½ tsp baking soda

½ cup (55 g) chopped pecans

½ cup (84 g) semi-sweet chocolate chips

½ cup (84 g) butterscotch morsels

Vanilla ice cream for serving, optional

Preheat the oven to 350°F (175°C) and lightly grease a 10-inch (25-cm) cast-iron skillet or 10-inch (25-cm) square baking pan.

In a large bowl or stand mixer, combine the softened butter, brown sugar and granulated sugar and mix well to combine. If using a stand mixer, mix on medium speed for this step. Whisk in the egg, then add the vanilla and mix well, either by hand or with your mixer set to low.

Stir in the flour, salt, cinnamon and baking soda. Mix until everything is combined.

Gently stir in the chopped pecans, chocolate chips and butterscotch morsels then spread the batter into the prepared pan and bake for 28 to 30 minutes, or until the edges are crispy and golden.

Let the skillet cool for 5 to 10 minutes before slicing.

Serve the cowboy cookie with vanilla ice cream, if desired. I highly recommend it!

MARGARITA KEY LIME PIE

Key lime pie is one of the most refreshing desserts. I put a little Texas spin on this one with the addition of tequila, Cointreau and sea salt. Why choose between a margarita and dessert when you can have both in one? A little slice of this topped with whipped cream is the ultimate treat or nightcap.

≳ Yield: 6–8 servings ≲

2 (14-oz [414-ml]) cans of sweetened condensed milk

4 egg yolks

½ cup (120 ml) Key lime juice

3 tbsp (45 ml) tequila

2 tsp (10 ml) Cointreau

Zest of 1 lime

Pinch of sea salt

1 (9-inch [23-cm]) premade graham cracker pie crust

Whipped cream, for topping

Lime wedges, for topping

Lime zest, for topping

Preheat the oven to 350°F (175°C).

In a medium mixing bowl, combine the sweetened condensed milk, egg yolks, Key lime juice, tequila, Cointreau, lime zest and sea salt. Whisk until the mixture is creamy and well combined, then pour the filling into the graham cracker pie crust.

Place the Key lime pie on a large baking sheet and transfer it to the oven. Bake for 20 minutes, or until the center is only slightly jiggly.

Let the pie cool for 30 minutes and then transfer it to the refrigerator to chill for 4 to 6 hours. The hardest part is waiting!

Cut the margarita Key lime pie into slices, serve with whipped cream, lime wedges and lime zest and dig in!

MEXICAN MARTINIS

Almost every Tex-Mex restaurant in Austin has a Mexican martini on the menu.
They are truly the best cocktail I have ever tasted. The key is good-quality reposado
tequila. They're a bit salty from the olive juice so a salt rim is very much optional.
However, I'm all for the salt rim and some extra olives.

Yield: 2 drinks

2 slices of lime

Sea salt for the rim, optional

3½ oz (105 ml) good-quality
reposado tequila

1½ oz (45 ml) Cointreau

1½ oz (45 ml) fresh lime juice

½ oz (15 ml) olive juice

Ice

Green olives

If you want a salt rim, run a lime slice around the rim of your glasses then
fill a shallow bowl or plate with salt. Gently dip the rim of each martini glass
in the salt to make a coated salt rim.

In a cocktail shaker, combine the tequila, Cointreau, lime juice, olive juice
and ice.

Give it a few good shakes then strain and pour it into the prepared martini
glasses.

Serve with some olives and a lime slice on the rim.

CUCUMBER-LIME MARGARITAS

Texas does a lot of things well. Tacos, BBQ, queso. But I think they do margaritas best. I've always been so inspired by the creativity of the restaurant scene in Austin when it comes to margaritas. I've had avocado, mango habanero and pineapple black pepper margaritas and they have all been delicious in their own special way. I love the refreshing combination of this cucumber lime version. This drink was made for a hot summer day.

⋛ Yield: 2 drinks ⋚

3 slices of lime

Sea salt

Ice

8 thin slices of cucumber, plus more for garnish

3 oz (90 ml) silver tequila

2 oz (60 ml) Cointreau

Juice from 1 lime

Lime seltzer water

Run one lime slice around the rim of your glasses. Fill a shallow bowl or plate with the sea salt. Gently dip the rim of the glass in the salt until it's coated. Add ice to the glasses then set aside.

Add the cucumber slices to a cocktail shaker and muddle them to release their juices. Fill the shaker with the tequila, Cointreau, lime juice and ice. Shake well to mix.

Divide the margarita between the two prepared glasses.

Add your desired amount of lime seltzer water to each glass (I use 2 to 3 ounces [60 to 90 ml] per glass). Garnish with a cucumber slice and a slice of lime.

SPICY PINEAPPLE MARGARITAS

A spicy margarita is a Texas specialty. I've had my fair share of fruity margaritas with a kick of spice. However, if there's pineapple available, that's what I'm getting! This homemade version is easy and only calls for a handful of ingredients. The chili lime salt rim is an absolute must!

⋛ Yield: 2 drinks ⋚

1 slice lime

½ tsp chili powder

½ tsp sea salt

4-6 jalapeño slices

Ice

6 oz (180 ml) pineapple juice

1 oz (30 ml) Cointreau

2 oz (60 ml) lime juice

3½ oz (105 ml) silver tequila

Pineapple slice or frond, for garnish, optional

Run a lime slice around the rim of your glasses. Fill a shallow bowl or plate with chili powder and sea salt and mix lightly to combine. Gently dip the rim of the glasses in the chili powder and salt to coat.

Muddle two to three jalapeño slices in the bottom of each prepared glass then top with ice.

In a cocktail shaker add more ice, along with the pineapple juice, Cointreau, lime juice and tequila. Shake well.

Pour into the prepared glasses. Garnish with a pineapple slice or frond for an extra pop, if desired.

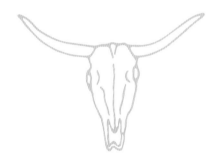

BOURBON SANGRIA

I have to give credit to Treaty Oak Distilling for this idea. It's a fun drinking spot in our little town that serves a bunch of fun cocktails, including a bourbon sangria. Don't knock it until you try it! Bourbon isn't typically my alcohol of choice. However, this sangria is my favorite drink that they make. I'm convinced Texans will add bourbon to just about anything.

Yield: 6 drinks

1 orange, thinly sliced

1 red apple, thinly sliced

6 oz (180 ml) bourbon

1 (25-oz [750-ml]) bottle of Cabernet Sauvignon

10 oz (300 ml) orange juice

8 oz (240 ml) seltzer water

Add the orange slices and apple slices to a large pitcher. Add the bourbon, Cabernet Sauvignon and orange juice to the pitcher.

Cover the pitcher loosely with a lid or clean dishtowel and refrigerate for 2 hours to let the flavors of the fruit develop.

Right before you are ready to serve, add the seltzer water. Pour the sangria in glasses with ice.

ACKNOWLEDGMENTS

Thank you, Robbie. Not only were you my taste tester for every recipe in this cookbook, but you also helped me develop a few of them! I couldn't have written this book without you. You're my number one fan and I can never thank you enough for cheering me on every single day. And for helping me with the dishes!

Thank you, Mom and Dad, for raising me to be someone who goes after what they want. Even if it's hard at first. I believe I'm a hard worker because I watched you both do it every day. My career choice may not be the most traditional, but you still believed in me from day one!

Thank you to the rest of my family and friends who let me vent about my workload and for your constant support! It means the world to me and I wish I could make you all tacos.

Thank you to everyone at Page Street Publishing for giving me this amazing and unforgettable opportunity. I'm so proud to be a cookbook author because of you!

And finally, to all the readers and followers of Dash of Mandi. I couldn't do this without you! I appreciate each and every one of you. Your support and excitement for me is what pushed me to keep going.

ABOUT THE AUTHOR

MANDI HICKMAN is the food blogger and photographer behind Dash of Mandi. Her creations are meant for busy people who want to make a homemade meal, but don't have hours to spend in the kitchen. They're no-fuss recipes that are packed with flavor. Mandi loves creating dishes inspired by a variety of cuisines but she especially loves Tex-Mex, thanks to her move to Austin in 2017.

When Mandi isn't creating new recipes in her kitchen, she's out exploring with her husband, Robbie, and dog, June—or relaxing on her back porch with a spicy margarita.

INDEX